A Woman's Guide
to a Better Marriage

SAM BRADLEY, PH.D.

© 2002 by Sam Bradley, Ph.D. All rights reserved.

No part of this book may be reproduced, stored in a retrieval system, or transmitted by any means, electronic, mechanical, photocopying, recording, or otherwise, without written permission from the author.

ISBN 0-7596-6592-3

This book is printed on acid free paper.

1stBooks – rev. 01/21/02

*She was my mentor,
now she is my guardian angel—*

in memory of Marian Wood Cannell.

ACKNOWLEDGEMENTS

When I came out of graduate school in 1973, specializing in interpersonal communication and clinical psychology, my head was full of theories about how people relate to one another. I thought I was pretty smart. Since then, I have met with hundreds of couples. Over the years, a dialogue has occurred between the theories I learned and the reality of people's needs. I would like to thank the many women and men who shared their heartaches with me, listened to my thoughts on marriage, tested my ideas, and came back to let me know what worked and what didn't. In school I learned other people's theories; from married women and men I learned the truth.

About 18 years ago, I sat in a small café in San Francisco with my buddy and colleague, Jim Ingersoll, and discussed how I had been working with couples. Jim started asking me clarifying questions. With each question my thinking got clearer and clearer about how a marital relationship is structured and how spouses really change the way they are going about being married so that success and fulfillment occurs. I owe a great debt of gratitude to Jim.

I also want to thank the many professionals who have taken my workshop, endearingly called, "Brief (No-Bullshit) Marital Therapy." Your questions and challenges to my ideas on commitment and fulfillment in marriage have helped fine-tune the advice in this book.

Thanks to Linda Gaffney for taking a raw writer and working and working until clear declarative sentences began to emerge. Linda helped edit my ideas into understandable English. Without her help, this book would not exist.

Thanks to Gorham Printing and Kathy Campbell for the cover design and formatting.

Many kind-hearted friends read preliminary manuscripts. Thanks to Gretchen Stangl-Charlton, James Scofield, Joan Scofield, Debra Squyres, and others who read, commented and helped create a better manuscript.

From my family I receive unconditional love. It is from this love that I draw encouragement and support, and so much of my feeling of fulfillment in life. It is a privilege to be the husband of my wife, Eileen, and the father of my daughter, Katie.

Olympia, Wa
March 2001

CONTENTS

Introduction: A Marriage Makeover—What to Expect/ 1

PART ONE: A Troubled Marriage
Marriage Makeover
Step 1: Accepting Your Starting Place / 9

PART TWO: The Anatomy of Marriage
Marriage Makeover
Step 2: Color Coding Your Marital Participation / 13

PART THREE: Reasonable and Rational Commitment
Marriage Makeover
Step 3: A Choice with Conditions / 18
Step 4: The Promise / 33
Step 5: Non-Iffy Love / 53
Step 6: Being Faithful / 56
Step 7: Your Commitment Mission Statement / 64

PART FOUR: Working on Success
Marriage Makeover
Step 8: Becoming an Action Valued Married Woman / 66
Step 9: Getting on Track Sexually / 92
Step 10: Surviving Set Backs / 102
Step 11: Knowing You are on Track / 113

PART FIVE: Marital Tips
Marriage Makeover

Step 12: De-Escalating Arguments / 118

Step 13: How to Apologize / 123

Step 14: Overcoming the Fear You Will Upset Him / 126

Step 15: Actions Speak Louder than Words / 136

Step 16: Deciding Household Tasks / 139

Step 17: Supporting Individual Interests / 145

Step 18: Being a Wife and a Mother / 149

Step 19: How to Maintain Romance / 152

PART SIX: Marital Problems or Mental Problems
Marriage Makeover

Step 20: Resolving—Is it We or Is it Me? / 155

PART SEVEN: Reaching Fulfillment
Marriage Makeover

Step 21: Being Your Best Self / 171

PART EIGHT: A Concluding Primer
Marriage Makeover

Step 22: An Overview / 186

INTRODUCTION: MARRIAGE MAKEOVER

What to Expect

MARRIAGE IS ONE OF THE MOST COMPELLING and challenging journeys you will ever undertake in life. It is a personal journey capable of providing tremendous interpersonal achievement as well as heartbreaking despair. If you hope to find success as a married woman, despite the inevitable difficulties of marriage, you must commit yourself to the journey, know what you need to do and how to do it effectively. By following the steps outlined in this book you can find out how to overcome a troubled marriage, feel pride, achieve success and find fulfillment from your own efforts as a married woman. By accomplishing the steps to a marriage makeover, you can achieve a more fulfilling marital experience. Doing a marriage makeover will be helpful to you if:

- You want to put an end to marital unhappiness.
- You know from experience that trying to change your husband to make marriage better does not work.
- You want to become a woman in charge of her own self-regard as a wife.
- You want to develop a personal guidance system that can lead to success and fulfillment.

- You want useful tips for making everyday marriage better.
- You want to resolve whether you are suffering from an emotional disorder or a marital problem.
- You want to realize your best self as a married woman—a place where self-actualization and authentic togetherness can occur.

It is my intention that the information here helps you find new ways of approaching roadblocks in your marriage; ways that can bring about increased hope and even renewed feelings of marital fulfillment. Knowing how to better your marital self from your own efforts can bring back confidence and self-regard, and save you from further marital heartbreak. I am going to tell you what you need to know to make being married work well for you by becoming a new and better marital self throught a marital makeover. And importantly, your marital makeover can make you feel better and more successful in marriage without any direct help from your husband.

IT'S ABOUT YOU, NOT YOUR HUSBAND

This is not a book about husbands, or about how to change your husband into a perfect mate. I am not going to tell you how to "make a new man out of him." I am not going to tell you that you can continue on with business as usual in your marriage and everything will be all right. I am not going to tell you it is all his fault. What I am going to do is tell you what you can do as a married woman to make marriage better for you. Will your changes help him? Sure, and that's okay. But the point is not to try to change him.

My basic belief is that you are in a position of great power as a married woman. You are in charge of yourself—your behaviors, your atti-

INTRODUCTION

tudes, and your emotions. Of course, your husband is in charge of himself as a husband, too, and so he is in a position of considerable power as well. Many women (and men) attempt to change their partner in the mistaken belief that "everything will be so much better if he would simply _____." You fill in the blank: Stop drinking, pay more attention to me, manage money better, keep his mother out of our business, be nicer to me, come home on time, take an anger management course. There are any number of ways a wife could wish her husband would change, and they are usually legitimate concerns. The problem with focusing on what your husband does—or does not do—is that you can't directly do anything about it. By focusing on issues that fall under your husband's control, you'll only produce helplessness and frustration on your part. You probably already know this: you can't change your husband by trying to change him. Best work on yourself and what you can do to feel better.

So, this book is not about husbands, but rather about how you can use knowledge and skill as a married woman to become more effective, more confident, and more in charge of yourself, even if your starting place is a troubled marriage. When you have acquired the wisdom and skills that make this happen, you will find you experience your marriage differently—and better. You will become better in your own terms; better at being married, independently from what your husband may or may not think about you as a wife. You will acquire a balance that comes from your being fully in charge of yourself in the marriage and your husband in charge of himself.

There will be no bad mouthing husbands in this book. There is no need for it. This is about you, and about how you can emerge from a troubled marriage, become successful at marriage, and feel good about yourself as a married woman. The most incredible relationship in life can occur between a wife and her husband. It's worth the effort to get the most out of it that you can.

MARITAL CHALLENGES

Unfortunately for many women, problems can become a marital way of life—difficulties that go on day after day. When this happens, marriage feels like a place of great despair, where hopes and desires crash against rigid marital walls. For these women, marriage is a confusing, hurtful, and often heartbreaking experience. Despite the discouraging problems in a difficult marriage, most women want to remain married. They want it to work; they want some of their dreams back; they do not want a divorce. They want a successful marital experience. They wonder what to do.

Some of the challenges that married woman wonder about may be familiar to you.

> My husband has been withdrawn from me for months. I'm so frustrated and hurt. I've even moved into the spare bedroom. Still, I don't want a divorce.
>
> My husband abuses alcohol. He stays out and drinks, comes home and is either belligerent or falls asleep. I've talked and talked, threatened and threatened. Nothing works.
>
> After five years of marriage, I have discovered that my husband engages in a behavior that I consider morally wrong and sick. He doesn't think so.
>
> My old high school sweetheart wants to have an affair with me. I'm feeling vulnerable.
>
> I don't feel like having sex with my husband anymore. He's done too many things lately that have hurt me.
>
> I feel out of control most of the time in my marriage. I know I'm reacting.

INTRODUCTION

When we argue, I feel like running. Sometimes I stay away for hours or even overnight. Most of our time together is good.

I'm afraid of saying what I think for fear it will upset my husband.

I feel frustrated about which one of us should do certain household tasks.

My husband wants to do something that I have a hard time imagining myself supporting.

Since the kids came along, it seems that I am a mother all the time and hardly ever a wife.

I feel so crazy in this marriage. Is it me or is it we? Do I suffer from a clinical disorder? Or, is the marriage making me feel this way?

I love my husband. I want to be more romantic, not just in big ways, but in little ways as well.

I want to experience confidence, pride and fulfillment as a married woman. How can I realize my higher self as a wife?

These are serious challenges for the married woman hoping to have a successful and fulfilling marital experience. Are there solutions? Yes, and every situation mentioned above will be addressed in the steps to a marital makeover.

THE PARTS OF THIS BOOK

In order to benefit the most from reading this book, I suggest that you start at the beginning and read each part as it unfolds. Ideas build on one another and new approaches and skills require clear reasons in order to be effective.

Part One is about accepting the difficult starting place for a marriage makeover. You will get to know Cheryl and her frustrating and heartbreaking marriage. Cheryl is in a seriously troubled marriage and doesn't know what to do. In a matter of months, she so changes the way she is going about being married that she begins to feel successful in her marriage. How Cheryl does this is a major theme throughout this book. You will learn in detail how she overcomes the heartbreak in her marriage, and eventually reaches fulfillment as a married woman, without any direct help from her husband, Ed.

Part Two is about how to choose the color for your marriage makeover. I explain the anatomy of marriage and how to effectively locate your role within the structure of marriage. You will learn the importance of the "color" of your "wife sphere," and about the marital "inbetween." Knowing the structure of your marriage and your "color" in it is essential for you to guide yourself successfully as a married woman.

Part Three is about commitment. A successfully married woman has a reasonable and rational view of commitment. She doesn't view marriage as being stuck, nor marital choice as unconditional. She has a perspective in place that gives her pride in herself and forms the basis for taking responsibility for her choice to be married and making marriage better. You will meet Sally, Darcy, and Karen who sorted out reasonable and rational views of commitment and gained an important sense of choice, condition, problem solving, fidelity, and love in being married. You may be surprised to find that I describe how Karen decided to get a divorce. For her, divorce was a reasonable and rational decision.

Part Four explains how to put in place a personal guidance sysem as part of your marriage makeover. It is about getting on track so that you can achieve fulfillment as a married woman. I believe a married woman hopes to achieve more than just the absence of problems in her

INTRODUCTION

marriage, but more importantly, she wants success and fulfillment. Getting on track is the way to success and fulfillment. You will learn how Cheryl got on track—how she struggled through her fears and confusion and got very good at managing her wife sphere and its "color"—independently of her husband's actions.

Part Five gives helpful marriage makeover tips ranging from how to de-escalate arguments, resolve resentments, apologize effectively, decide household tasks, separate being a wife from being a mother, and how to maintain romance. You will meet married women who learned about these tips and tried them out.

Part Six addresses the question of whether you have an emotional problem that is blocking your progress toward fulfillment as a married woman, or whether your emotionality is coming from the troubled marriage you are in. I will explain how to determine whether you have an emotional problem or emotionally troubled marriage. You will meet Nancy, who overcame an obsessive-compulsive disorder, and Tricia, who resolved the effects of sexual abuse, so each could get on track in their marriages.

In **Part Seven**, I describe how the higher self, fulfillment and the "interhuman" will occur as you accomplish your marriage makeover. Did Cheryl get there? Yes, and I will describe to you how she did it.

Finally, **Part Eight** concludes with an overview of what a married woman needs to know to achieve a marriage makeover.

AUTHOR BIASES

There are many ways of viewing a marital relationship and a married woman's participation in it. I tend to be very "here-and-now" and pragmatic. I have seen married women overcome nearly every imaginable obstacle and go on to be married successfully. They have not had to go back and rework their family of origin, they have not had to resolve unconscious motives for choosing their partner, they have not had to analyze and journal their dreams, they have not had to sort out female and male energy and which planet they come from, they have not had to analyze their parents' marriage, they have not had to figure out which of the four horsemen of the apocalypse they are, and they have not had to become a self-trained behavioral or solution-focused therapist to their husband or their marriage to feel good about themselves as married women.

What a woman needs to know is how to conceptualize herself as a participant in her marriage, and how to manage her participation in order to do it well in her own terms. When women know how to guide themselves successfully in marriage, they are remarkably successful at being married. Marital solutions are in the future and it is what you are going to do today and tomorrow that will shape your marital satisfaction, not what you did yesterday. Overall my bias is this: If you are not knowledgeable about how to be married and you don't know how to do it well, then marriage will be a confusing and troublesome experience. On the other hand, if you understand the anatomy of a marital relationship, how to rationally and reasonably conceptualize commitment, and how to become an action valued married woman, you are likely to do a good job of being married, and as a consequence, experience marital satisfaction and fulfillment as a married woman.

Marriage, as we move into the 21st Century, is about choice, responsibility, equality, and fulfillment. If you feel you want a marriage with these essential qualities, you should follow the steps I present and do a marriage makeover.

PART ONE: A TROUBLED MARRIAGE

MARRIAGE MAKEOVER

STEP ONE

Accepting Your Starting Place

*Are you frustrated and unhappy in your marriage?
Maybe you have some of the same struggles
Cheryl had in her marriage.*

CHERYL CAME TO MY OFFICE FEELING SAD, angry and hopeless about her marriage. She had been married to Ed for five years. The last year of marriage had been awful. It is her second marriage, his first. She's 32 years old with two children—one from her first marriage and one with Ed. She works as an elementary school teacher. One child is in the third grade and the other is in day care. Because she loves Ed and because of the children, the failure of her marriage breaks her heart. She had such great hopes.

The first few years were wonderful. Ed seemed to enjoy being with Cheryl whether they were just sitting holding hands in the family room, or out on the town with friends. He was romantic and attentive. Marriage was great. Then, just over a year ago, Ed's asphalt paving business took a downturn. Construction had been pretty good but when area development slowed, his crews were barely able to keep busy. Ed withdrew from Cheryl and the children, spending long hours at his office, and on the phone at home. When he wasn't working he wanted to be left alone to sit and watch television. Cheryl, Ed and the kids ate meals together, but there was little or no conversation. Time together diminished, attention lessened, and romance faded. Their sexual relationship stopped altogether. Cheryl finally moved into a separate bedroom when she could no longer stand the coldness of Ed's rigid posture in their bed.

When I asked Cheryl to describe her situation, she said, "I've tried everything. Nothing works. I try to get him to talk about his feelings, he won't. He withdraws. I've gotten frustrated and yelled at him. I've felt hopeless and pleaded with him to talk with me, to let me know what I can do, to be close to me again. Nothings works. I've withdrawn into myself. I don't even do nice things for him, anymore. I've tried everything. Now, I've just given up. I work, take care of the kids, watch TV and sleep in my own room. He stays in his space and I stay in mine. We are not even good roommates! It's terrible—he refuses to come to marital therapy with me. He just says he won't. I don't know what to do to try to make this marriage last. I think about divorce all the time now. I'm lost."

Ed's refusal to come to counseling hurt and angered her. She even threatened to leave him if he did not get help, but the more she tried, the more he withdrew. It seemed the harder she tried the worse it got.

Cheryl had been doing her best to endure for months, and by the time she turned up in my office for help, she was feeling completely disheartened. No longer her old cheerful self, Cheryl had withdrawn too, and had begun to wonder if she was clinically depressed. Her thoughts were more and more often about hopelessness and divorce. She no longer tried to interest Ed in her activities. She had stopped trying to be affectionate and sexual. She spent her days going to work, taking care of the children, and spending a little time with her friends. She didn't know what she could do. She was confused, dejected and ready to give up.

Cheryl was bringing more than a year's worth of hurt, anguish and anger to my office that day. There was more than a little bit of confusion, guilt and blame, too. She had struggled with ideas about how to mend

ACCEPTING YOUR STARTING PLACE

her broken marriage. She had mentally given herself deadlines for making something change. She had reached out to the resources of friends and family in order to find the support and comfort needed to keep going in the face of this difficult time. She had not given up without trying, that's for sure. Cheryl did not lack effort and persistence. She had, however, been working at the problem of repairing her marriage from a place where she had little power to effect changes, and thus had been experiencing frustration and distress. She had honest questions about what to do next. There was nothing she could do to change her husband. His unwillingness to seek counseling was a major frustration for her. His unwillingness to talk with her about their problems devastated her. Cheryl stated she felt lost, frustrated and nearly hopeless, but she also told me she didn't want a divorce. She'd had one marriage that didn't work out and knows how hurtful divorce can be. I kept thinking to myself as I heard Cheryl tell her story, "She needs to know what she can do for herself as a wife in this marriage. She's not in charge of Ed, or of what Ed does about being married, but she *can be* in charge of herself. There is a lot Cheryl can do about her marriage, a lot she hasn't thought of, doesn't know and hasn't done. If only she knew how, Cheryl could be in charge of new ways of approaching the problems in her marriage, ways that can bring about new hope and perhaps even renewed feelings of marital fulfillment."

Cheryl is not alone. Despite the many disdainful remarks about marriage which emanate from people in all walks of life in our society, most of us want to be married. We value marriage. We want to be in a close and loving marital relationship and to feel good about ourselves. Marriages "go awry" for a lot of different reasons. When they do, most of us don't know what to do, or how to do it—especially when a marriage goes sour to the extent Cheryl's has. Ed was not having an affair, or being physically abusive. He had not gambled away the family fortune, or shown deep disregard for the welfare and safety of his children. Cheryl's marriage had gone awry because both she and Ed lessened their marital involvement until not much of what could be called "marriage" remained. Marriage ceased to exist in any meaningful way. Cheryl wanted to remain married to Ed. What was she to do?

I am convinced that if women like Cheryl knew what to do to improve their marital experience, they would do it. More than half of first time marriages eventually end in divorce. Many of these marriages end because either the woman or the man don't know how to be married well. They simply lack the knowledge and skills to know how to make a marriage work successfully. Others end because they don't know what to do when their marriage gets into trouble. They get along for the most part, but when problems come up they don't know how to do the necessary repair work. They get stuck in the despair of their own making and don't know how to get back on track. Marriage can be a huge part of a person's life and I could see Cheryl wanted a better marriage, not a divorce.

Cheryl found ways of being married that brought her success and fulfillment, and a better marriage. In a matter of months, without direct efforts to alter Ed's behavior, Cheryl so changed the way she was going about being married, that she brought about a new and fulfilling sense to her experience of being married to Ed. Knowing how to be married differently brought confidence, pride and fulfillment back to Cheryl's life as a wife. How did she do this? After describing some important ideas about marriage, I'm going to take you step-by-step through the ideas and skills that Cheryl developed as she made her marriage a successful experience for her, and of other married women as well. As we go through Cheryl and other wives' experiences together, you will learn how to accomplish your own marriage makeover.

PART TWO: THE ANATOMY OF MARRIAGE

MARRIAGE MAKEOVER

STEP TWO

Color Coding Your Marital Participation

Do you know the anatomy of your marriage and the how your participation interacts with Marriage/Husband?

THE ANATOMY OF MARRIAGE

JUST AS IT HELPS TO KNOW SOME HUMAN ANATOMY when you exercise, or the identity of spices when you cook, or some accounting terms if you do taxes, it helps to know the parts of marriage when you want to emerge from a troubled marriage and have a successful one. What are the different roles in a marriage? How are they related to each other? What are the limitations of the marital roles? What is the best to expect of individual and combined roles? Knowing the structure of marriage gives you invaluable insights about your sphere in the marriage, your potential and limitations, how to solve difficulties and how to go about being married successfully.

THE WEDDING

Remember your wedding ceremony? The structure of marriage all began with your wedding. Understanding your wife sphere begins with an appreciation of the ceremony that created it. At the time of your wedding you were probably focused on the moment. You didn't realize that your wedding ceremony was a transformational ritual. That you were participating in a process that created your wife sphere, his husband sphere, and a mutual sphere called marriage. By participating in your wedding you made yourself a married woman—a wife. Becoming a wife was a choice you made at the time of your wedding—being a wife is a choice you make everyday of your marital life. According to an old Chinese saying: Others can open the door but only you can walk through it.

Through the wedding ceremony you created your wife sphere, your husband created his husband sphere, and as a wife and a husband to each other, you collectively created the marital sphere in a place called the inbetween.

THE MARITAL INBETWEEN

Your marriage occurs in a place between you and your husband where the interpersonal existence of your marriage resides. This is your marital inbetween. This inbetween is made up of what you put into it through your participation as a wife, and what your husband puts into it through his participation as a husband. Your participation and his get mixed together in this middle place where your being as a wife and his being as a husband meet—where you both make your marriage and sustain it. Your inbetween space is filled up by your participation as spouses and forms your marriage.

COLOR CODING YOUR SPHERE

While the marital inbetween, where your marriage exists, is made up of what each of you put into it as spouses, it is more than the sum of your mutual participation. Think of it as colors. Say, you put into the marital inbetween a lovely shade of yellow and your husband puts in a stunning blue, your marriage would be a vibrant green. Your yellowness and his blueness create the greenness. The greenness could not exist without the yellow color of your participation and his blue colored participation—but as green it has its own unique identity. The marital inbetween is a mixture of yellow and blue. The marriage is green. Interestingly, neither you nor your husband is able to make the green occur by her or himself—you are limited to your yellow, and he is restricted to his blue, if you want green. If "green" is a successful marriage, then the most you can do to obtain it, is to make sure you are being a married woman who sustains her color of yellow as a wife. All your power comes from being your color as a wife and what you put into the marital inbetween through your participation in it. All your power comes from your color. If you want a green marriage and your color is yellow, you must put in yellow—your sphere must be the best and most vibrant yellow color you can make it. That's the most you can do to have green. Conversely, your husband must put in blue, if he wants a green marriage. But, what if he doesn't?

Let's say he changes and begins putting into the marital inbetween brown and in reaction to his brown you put in red. Your marriage would change to a muddy purple. Now, suppose this purple is an awful marriage. You don't like this purple marriage; it hurts to be in this purple marriage. You try to change him, to get him to go back to putting in his color of blue. Unfortunately, the more you try to change him, the redder you get and probably the browner he becomes. At this point, despite who started it, you are both responsible for creating purple, the miserable marriage. You decide that you don't like this mucky purple marriage, so you try to change it to green by going back to yellow. No matter what he does, you put in your yellow. Whatever color he chooses will combine with your yellow color and whatever is produced will at least have the potential for green in it. Maintaining the yellow color of your wife sphere produces the opportunity for greenness to reoccur should he go back to his blueness. Without the presence of your yellow, there is no chance of green occurring. And, you discover that it feels good to be yellow and not red. This book will explain to you how to choose the color of your wife sphere and the value of sticking to it.

Because of the structure of marriage, there are certain truths about your wife sphere and the inbetween of your marriage:

- Being a married woman is a choice you are making. Nobody can make you be a wife but you.
- You are in charge of your actions—your color—your wife sphere—as a married woman.
- You are never in charge of your husband's sphere—his color—in the marriage, only he is.
- He is never in charge of your sphere—your color—in the marriage, only you are.
- He can make it hard or easy for you to put what you want into the marital inbetween—be the wife you want to be—your color—but he will never be in charge of it.
- You can make it hard or easy for him to put what he wants into the marital inbetween—be the husband he wants to be—his color—but you will never be in charge of it.
- Putting the best of your character—your color—into the

marital inbetween is what you can do to increase the quality of your marriage.
- The most you can do about anything at any given moment in your marriage comes from the color you choose to be as a married woman—the color of your wife sphere.

A lot of advice follows based on the structure of marriage I just explained. Keep one thing in mind as we go along: You are in charge of whether you are a married woman. You are also in charge of what you are like as a wife. Your choice to be a married woman and what you are like as a wife are in your domain, they are part of the color you choose to be, and they always will be. Knowing the structure I have just explained is essential for you to know who you are, how to put together the wife sphere you want, and how to find success as a married woman. Your wife sphere is your starting place for getting to success. From here on out consider yourself to have your own particular and unique wife sphere. I will help you choose your best color as we go along.

PART THREE:
REASONABLE & RATIONAL COMMITMENT

MARRIAGE MAKEOVER

STEP THREE

A Choice With Conditions

Do you want to be married to your husband?
How does a reasonable and rational
woman view commitment?

THE ADULT CHOICE to be married forms the very foundation of being married successfully. There is no middle ground in being married or not. You are either married and a wife or you are not. If you are choosing to be married, you are a married woman. While you may think of divorce a lot, if you have not initiated the legal process to get a divorce, you are choosing to be married. One of the basic premises of this book is that, as an adult woman choosing to be married you want to make it work. It will never make sense to choose to be married and then go about it in a way that doesn't work.

Let me draw it out a bit so that the fullness of your choice becomes clearer. As we have seen, before your marriage ceremony, you were a single woman. On you wedding day, you chose to become a married woman. The choice to be married is not just a choice only on your wedding day, it is a choice every day of your married life. I like to tell married couples, "nobody can make you be married but you," in order to empha-

A CHOICE WITH CONDITIONS

size the adult responsibility that goes with this choice. To make this logic apply to you, personally, let me ask you a question. This question is deceptively simple but far reaching in its implications for your marriage. The question is: **Do you want to be married to your husband?**

The answer to this rather obvious but important question begins the work of making your experience as a married woman successful and fulfilling.

There are three possible answers to the question of whether you want to be married to your husband: "No," "Maybe," and "Yes." Let's explore each of these answers so you will know how they apply to your choice to be married or not.

NO, I DON'T WANT TO BE MARRIED

The simplest answer is "no." If you are so clear about your intentions that your answer is "no" then call an attorney. You are choosing not to be a married woman, and to be married no longer. No one can make you be married, so if this is your choice, do it. This is a book that holds individual choice as central to making life meaningful for you; it is not a book that strives to save all marriages no matter what. Divorce is painful enough without having someone who does not know your circumstances, judging you. You are an adult woman and if you do not choose to be married to your husband anymore, by all means take the steps necessary to stop being a wife and get a divorce.

I recently asked the, "Do you want to be married?" question to a wife and husband who had come to my office to explore their troubled marriage. He answered, "Yes." She answered, "No." She didn't waver, or say that she didn't know for sure, she was clear about her marital state of mind and said, "No." While she was clear about not wanting to be married to her husband any longer, she had not begun the legal process of getting a divorce. She was still living in a state of marriage with him. At her husband's urging, she had agreed to go to counseling, thinking since he had requested it, she should do it for his sake. This resulted in her sending him a double message. She was continuing to live with him, not getting a divorce but intending to, while agreeing to attend counseling. He concluded, quite logically, that she must still want to be married, if only their problems could be resolved. But, in my office, when I asked the question, "Do you want to be married to your husband?" she answered, "No."

The answer to the question helped her communicate clearly and precisely where she stood. While he was stunned, he heard her. Her clarity helped establish a reality for him, which he had to begin accepting—a woman who did not plan to be married to him any longer. He needed and deserved to know this so that he could begin the adjustment process to this new reality. As is the case with most adults, he will adjust to reality better than to what he thinks, fears, or imagines to be real.

Sitting with the couple, I decided to play devil's advocate with her, to determine how clear she was about getting a divorce, and so her husband could begin to hear that clarity. I made it pretty dramatic so there would be no shadow in his mind, and none in hers. "What if your husband got cancer, and had only six months to live? What if he got into a serious auto accident, was incapacitated and needed a home in which to recover—what if he couldn't sign his own legal documents? What if he lost his job and had no money and no place to live? I laid it on thick and heavy, just to be sure we got to the heart of her decision.

How did she respond? She said, "I really hope none of that happens. I would feel horrible if it did. Larry doesn't deserve any awful tragedies in his life. But, it would be false for me to stay married. I can't be married and not have any of the feelings I need. I don't love Larry anymore. I've tried to get the feelings back for a long time, but they aren't there. I would be a fake if I tried to be his wife under any circumstances."

Her husband was heartbroken and wanted to know why she had agreed to go to counseling with him. "Why haven't you told me you want a divorce? Why have you led me on like this, agreeing to go to counseling?" he asked. He thought they had been coming for marriage counseling, and now it was turning out to be divorce counseling. He was angry, and he was hurt beyond words. She told him that she was sorry he felt misled, that she hadn't wanted to hurt him, but "nobody has ever asked me so directly whether or not I want to be married or not, and I don't."

With this last statement, he heard her and it became clear to him that he must prepare himself for divorce. We agreed that he would continue to see me in therapy while she would get on with the legal paperwork. Today, he is getting his life organized without her, resolving his hurt feelings and adjusting okay.

MAYBE, I WANT TO BE MARRIED

Another answer you may have to the question of whether you want to be married to your husband is "maybe." I've talked to a lot of wives over the years who answered, "Maybe." Sometimes being married is so difficult, so dissatisfying, and a such a miserable overall experience, that you think a lot about getting a divorce. You don't feel like being married, and sometimes you don't even feel you ARE married. While you may not feel married and you think about divorce, if you haven't actually called a lawyer, if you have filed no papers, if you haven't told your husband you intend to get a divorce, and if you haven't gotten your life started off in a new, single direction, YOU ARE STILL MARRIED!

There is no middle ground in marriage. You are either a married woman choosing to be a wife, or you are not. There isn't even a word in the English language, or other languages of which I am aware, for "kind-of-being-a-married woman-but-not-really." Sometimes you may think that if you are separated, you are not really a married woman. Wrong.

You are a wife who is separated from her husband.

It is important to recognize that you are making a choice by staying in the marriage, by not getting a divorce, even if you think about divorce on a regular basis. This recognition of the fact of choice allows you to take responsibility for your decision. Taking responsibility helps you fully realize that if a choice is being made then it is best to get on with making the choice a successful one for you. If the choice is to get a divorce, make that direction work as best it can for you. If the choice is to be married, make that direction work as best it can for you. It will never make sense to choose to be married (not get a divorce), and then go about being married in ways that cannot be successful. When you answer "Maybe" you are attempting to fashion a middle ground that doesn't exist, thus creating a place from which success as a married or single woman is impossible.

Divorce is both a psychological and a legal process. It is another one of society's transformational rituals that enables a woman to end her role as a wife and begin a new life being single. (I deplore the term "ex" when applied to a former spouse, either wife or husband. It seems incredibly negative to define a person by what they once were, but no longer are.) While society expects you to wait until your divorce is legal to call yourself single again, I think that psychologically divorce begins when you decide no longer to be married, when you tell your husband you are no longer going to be married to him, and begin creating a single life. If you are not declaring yourself to be psychologically and legally getting a divorce—in other words, saying "No" to marriage—then you are still married. There is no marital place called, "maybe." If you are saying "Maybe," I challenge you to take responsibility for the choice you are making to remain married, and make being married successful.

A CHOICE WITH CONDITIONS

YES, I WANT TO BE MARRIED

Returning to the question "Do you want to be married to your husband?" we have come to the final possible answer. If you have answered "Yes" then you are clearly choosing to be married. You are acknowledging that nobody can make you be married but you, and that you are choosing to take responsibility for your decision to be a married woman. While it is obvious that there are many difficult trade-offs in marital situations, the bottom line will always be that you are an adult woman choosing to be married. Whatever the trade-offs of your particular situation—and I know some of them can be difficult—the only way to begin guiding yourself toward success in marriage is to recognize that you are married by choice. Marital repair work and efforts to be married successfully, begin with your rational adult decision to be a wife.

MARITAL CONDITIONS

What were your marital vows? Do you remember the promises you made when you got married? In a very compelling moment in your life, you stood with your partner, in front of some official person—a minister, priest, rabbi, or judge—and repeated certain vows, or promises. These days, a lot of people are writing their own vows, so perhaps the words you spoke on that day were ones that you had chosen just for that occasion. Traditionally, though, the wedding vows contain some kind of promise that you (the bride) will take this man to be your lawfully wedded husband forever. Some weddings contain the phrasing, "to have and to hold from this day forward, for better for worse, for richer for poorer, in sickness and health, until death do us part." Marital vows that state you must stay together forever are lovely sentiments, and it would be nice if simply expressing these words would make marriages last until death but it doesn't work that way: thinking that because you are married, anything goes, does not work. So, please do not take these vows literally. There is a better way to express commitment, one that supports a successful marriage between two adults, so why not bring a clearly reasonable and rational form of commitment to your marriage?

If you think I am being pessimistic about marriage, or that I am saying your marriage vows are of little value, please let me explain. I believe marriage is a reasonable adult activity. Vows of commitment for "forever no matter what," mean that you can do anything you want and your husband has to stay with you. Do you think this is true? Unconditional vows of forever also mean that he can do anything he wants, and you have to stay with him. Is this true as well? Eternal vows literally commit you to an unconditional relationship. Eternal vows mean that if you are married you are stuck. Without condition, you must stay married, no matter what. But adults do not enter into unconditional relationships, not even in marriage. To commit to marriage for life no matter what he does or you do, is an irrational idea. Irrational ideas do not fit well in successful marriages.

Regrettably, many adults go about the business of being married as though they are in an unconditional relationship that cannot end. They act as though they can do anything and their spouse has to remain married to them. Under this umbrella of unconditionality, I have seen spouses ignore, spit on, swear at, lie to, cheat, physically abuse, torture their children, and act totally indifferent to one another. I have seen spouses endure all this because they are married. The unconditional idea of commitment, while not necessarily resulting in such despicable acts, has no place in a healthy marriage. You can't be married successfully if you think "Anything goes!" and your marriage will just keep rolling along. Adults do not suspend their rationality at the door of marriage. Reason and reasonableness must still prevail in marriage as in all adult activities if success is the goal. Sensible adults in all walks of

A CHOICE WITH CONDITIONS

life and all religions find ways of ending marriages if unacceptable conditions occur. They recognize that there are behaviors so abhorrent to human relations, and so hurtful, that it is not merely unreasonable, but also irrational, to stay married.

For instance, I got a call one evening from a woman who told me that her husband had severely beaten her. She was afraid that he would kill her if she called the police. We outlined a plan for her immediate safety and I called the police. The police responded quickly, and found her seriously injured. The husband was arrested. Medical examination showed the woman had a broken sternum, a broken cheekbone, one eye swollen shut, and her face was horribly bruised and puffy. Investigations revealed a history of abuse, but never as extreme as that night. Should this woman have stayed in her marriage for life and endured abuse because she said she would? Was this the life she agreed to when she took her vows and said, "I do?" This woman got into therapy, began to understand the dynamics of abuse, gave her husband the opportunity to get treatment which he refused, rebuilt her sense of self-worth, and got a divorce.

Both spouses had been acting out a marriage built around the idea that their relationship was unconditional. He acted as though he could do whatever he wanted—even physically injure her—and she would have to stay with him because they were married. She acted as though she had to endure whatever he did—even beat her up—because she was married. When she understood and accepted that marriages are conditional relationships—that reason does not stop at the door to marriage—she got a divorce. It was no longer rational for her to remain married to him. He "helped" with her decision by blaming her for his abuse, refusing to accept responsibility for his actions, and refusing to get help. In every instance where I have interviewed a couple who is experiencing abuse in their marriage, I have found the idea buried in their marital attitudes that marriage is unconditional—it is forever no matter what, so I can do whatever I want, or I have to endure whatever happens. I have come to the conclusion that healthy marriages know commitment has its conditional limits based on rational-decision making.

Of course, there are less extreme examples of the conditional nature of relationships. When I wrote a newspaper column on marriage some years ago, a woman responded to the idea of conditions in marriage this way: "I left my husband of 43 years because he was an alcoholic. He had many chances to stop drinking, and he never did. I am very happy now, and basically feel that I did the only reasonable thing in getting a divorce. However, over the years I have felt guilty. Like I didn't have the right to get a divorce because I was breaking the marriage vows, 'in sickness and in health, for better or for worse, till death do us part.' You said something in your column that no one else has said. Marriage is conditional. I am a reasonable adult woman. I didn't give that up when I got married. Thank you."

This woman felt she had done something wrong by divorcing her chronically alcohol abusing husband. She felt guilty. When she viewed herself as a rational and reasonable woman with conditions for whether she will be a married woman or not, she felt better about herself, as she should. She had conditions, she got a divorce, she acted rationally.

But what kind of conditions might a women have for being a wife or not? What are wives baseline reasons for getting a divorce? I ask all married woman who come to my office for help with their marriage about their conditions for being married. My question is: "What is something that if your husband did it, you would consider it a rational and reasonable act to stop being a wife and get a divorce?" I typically ask this question with the husband present. (I also ask the husband the same respective question.) As you can imagine, husbands are quite alert when this question is asked. Wives have shared with me many rational

A CHOICE WITH CONDITIONS

reasons for getting a divorce. One said typically, "I would get a divorce if my husband lost all feelings for me. If he stopped caring and he felt no love for me. I wouldn't be able to endure that. It wouldn't make sense for me to be married to a man who just didn't care for me. Besides, I don't think I would be treated very well by a husband who didn't care. It would be awful."

Another said: "I would get a divorce if my husband became an addict—drugs, alcohol, gambling—and refused to get help and it went on and on. I'd stick with him if he got help, but if he refused to try to change, it wouldn't make any sense to stay married. I don't think you have to be a masochist or a martyr to be married. That doesn't make sense to me."

Universally, wives have said to me: "If my husband physically or sexually abused our children, I would get a divorce." I ask them if it would make a difference if he got help with his abuse problem. The wives tell me, "I'm not sure that would make a difference. Maybe. I'd have to know it would definitely never happen again. Without that reassurance, I'd get a divorce."

Wives also typically mention philandering as a condition: "If my husband had sex with other women and wouldn't stop, I'd get a divorce." A woman I talked with on the phone recently related that her husband was having an affair. She found out when she was eight months pregnant that her husband's girl friend was also eight months pregnant, and expecting twins. Although it was a difficult time in her life, she got a divorce.

When asked, wives express good reasons for getting a divorce. They are very serious about conditions and do not take them lightly. They know that if conditions such as those above were to occur, it would make no sense to remain married. Marriage would be a miserable experience with no hope for a successful one to evolve.

CONDITIONS AND ULTIMATUMS

While I ask wives who come to my office about the conditions that would prompt them to leave their marriage, I make a distinction between a condition and an ultimatum. Conditions have a place in healthy marriages; ultimatums do not.

Suppose a wife goes to her husband and wags her finger in his face and tells him she will leave him unless he stops drinking. This is an ultimatum. Ultimatums are attempts to control the husband's behavior by threatening to leave. The focus of a condition is not on the husband's behavior but on the wife's choice to be married; what she will endure and not endure as a married woman. A conversation that Helen had with her husband, Bill, about his drinking, shows how Helen invoked a condition rather than an ultimatum

Bill had been going to his favorite tavern after work and coming home later and later for months. When he got home, he was usually drunk. All he wanted to do was eat and go to sleep. Sometimes he fell asleep on the couch, and sometimes in bed. At times, he berated Helen if dinner was not ready, or if she objected to his drinking, he called it nagging. Recently, Bill had gotten a ticket for driving while intoxicated. While he kept his job, Helen knew that his work performance was poor, and there were occasional days when he didn't go to work at all. As he drank more, finances began to suffer. One Saturday afternoon, when Bill was not drinking, and activities around the house were calm, Helen said to Bill, "I want to talk to you about something really important to me, so please listen. It is about your drinking. I'll just say this once and then you can think about it. It's because I love you that I'm saying this. I want our marriage to last."

Bill leaned against the kitchen table and nodded his head. "Okay," he said. Helen looked directly at Bill and said, "I'm not in charge of your alcohol use, you are. I'm not responsible for whether you decide to do something about it, you are. I'm responsible for whether I stay married to someone who abuses alcohol and doesn't stop. I know that if I stay married to you like this, I will eventually lose all my feelings for you, and I don't want that to happen. I'd rather deal with it now. I'm not telling you what you have to do; you can do whatever you want. You're an adult. I'm telling you that I won't be married to someone who abuses alcohol and doesn't try to stop. It's a choice I am making for myself. Bill, I hope you hear this."

Bill took a couple of gulps of air. Helen had never talked to him like this. He could tell that she was serious. "I'll give it some thought," he said.

Helen did a good job of applying a condition to her choice of whether to be married to someone abusing alcohol, and not to his behavioral choices as an adult. Her choice about whether to be a wife or not resides in her domain of decisions affected by her standards concerning what she will and, will not, endure. She recognizes that she would "lose all her feelings" for Bill if she continued in the marriage as it was, and to wait for that would make no sense to her. She was also careful to remember that Bill has a range of choices in his domain of decision-making as a husband. Helen is making a choice about what she does, and not about what Bill will do. She cannot make him drink or stop drinking. Only Bill can decide what he will do, and only Bill can do it. Thus, Helen wisely stayed in her domain and applied rational criteria to her choice of whether to remain in her marriage with Bill. No one can make her be a wife, and her choice of whether to be one with Bill includes some reasonable conditions. The bottom line is: Helen is not responsible for whether Bill abuses alcohol, but she is responsible for the choice she makes in continuing to be married to someone who engages in alcoholic behavior, and does nothing about it.

What happened to Helen and Bill? What do you predict? I am interested in what women believe happens in this kind of situation where a married woman sorts out reasonable standards for her choice, applies it to herself, treats her partner as adult responsible for his choices, and communicates it to him as an expression of a personal condition and not an ultimatum. Risking a prediction sometimes draws out hidden beliefs about being a wife and being married. Look into your mind now and see what you are thinking happened to Helen and Bill.

For a few weeks Bill stopped going to the tavern after work, and he came home sober every night. Helen was pleased. She enjoyed those few weeks. It seemed that Bill was enjoying this time as well. Then, Bill was late one night and Helen got a call from the jail. Bill had gotten another DUI! Helen picked him up and brought him home. The next day she filed for divorce, and Bill was served papers a few days later. He was astounded! Despite the clarity of Helen's message when she had talked to him about her conditions for remaining married, Bill was shocked to receive divorce papers.

Then, partly through the process of taking care of his DUI charge, which required him to face his alcoholism in the larger arena of the court system, and partly on his own initiative, Bill entered treatment. Helen kept her word about remaining in the marriage if he got help, and she suspended the divorce proceedings. Bill went on to complete treatment and, two years later, Helen and Bill are still married. Bill attends AA meetings, takes his choice to remain sober seriously, and Helen is enjoying her marriage to him. Would Helen have divorced herself from Bill had he not stopped drinking? I think she would have, Helen believes she would have, and Bill thinks she would have. Helen knew the heartache of being married to an alcoholic, and she became committed to having a successful marriage, or none at all.

Sometimes, a wife may answer my "condition question," in a way that might sound trivial. An example would be Angela, whose initial statement was: "If I can't get him to stop spending so much time on the

A CHOICE WITH CONDITIONS

Internet." With a bit of probing, however, Angela gave me the history of Jeff's relationship to the Internet. He had two computers set up in his home office, "war room" as he called it, and each was equipped with a modem for Internet access. He had forbidden Angela to go into this room, but she had gained entry anyway. She found the walls of his private room covered with pornographic pictures. Every evening, Jeff would be in two "chat" rooms simultaneously, exchanging electronic intimacies with women across the world. Jeff usually rolled into bed past 2:00 a.m. with no sexual energy left and no interest in Angela. They had not made love in two years. Angela's original remark might have seemed frivolous, but given Jeff's obsessive behaviors, her real concern was rational and reasonable. Angela then had to decide whether she faced a condition or a problem to solve with Jeff. She chose to treat it as a problem to address.

If you want a successful marriage, commit yourself to the principle that your participation is a choice, and that your choice is guided by rational and reasonable conditions. These conditions would apply no matter whom you had married—in other words, they are not simply something you've dreamed up to make your husband's life miserable. Integrate into your self-concept the orientation that you are a reasonable and rational adult woman with conditions for whether or not you will remain a wife. Allow this thinking to settle deeply within your ideas about your marital self. Knowing that you bring reasonable conditions to your choice to be married will help you take into your marriage a healthy notion of yourself as a prideful and confident person.

Do married women have unreasonable conditions? No, I have never had a married woman share with me frivolous conditions for continuing in a marriage. No one has ever said, "I think it would be reasonable for me to get a divorce if he doesn't pick up after himself," or, "he watches too much TV." These can be irritating behaviors, but they are not conditions. Wives aren't superficial in their commitment, they are serious and have a right to reasonable conditions for their choice of whether to remain married. Sometimes, husbands do not see conditions the same way as wives do. Bill thought Helen was overreacting to his drinking until she sorted out her conditions and expressed them to him as a commentary on her and not him. He tested her sincerity and found out she was serious. When husbands hear conditions expressed they may object, deny, minimize, and test but they know they are dealing with something different from nagging or ultimatums. Conditions are serious and for real.

Reading about conditions has no doubt made you think of what yours would be. Ask yourself the question, "What is something, that if my husband were to do it, it would be reasonable and rational for me to choose to stop being married (get a divorce), and unreasonable and irrational for me to choose to remain married?" Write down the three or four conditions that come to mind. This will help you clarify that you are choosing to be in a conditional relationship in your marriage—a healthy acknowledgement.

MARRIAGE MAKEOVER
STEP FOUR

The Promise

You are going to have problems in your marriage. Everyone does. When you commit to being married, what is the most reasonable and rational promise to make toward problem solving?

PROBLEMS ARE PART OF THE MARITAL TERRITORY—if you are married, you are going to have problems. For example, Mary had a problem in her marriage when her husband, Barry, decided he did not want to have children and she did. This was a huge problem; one that could end their marriage. Aaron and Sarah disagreed about food. Sarah was a vegetarian but Aaron was not. Planning meals at home and finding a suitable restaurant when eating out were ongoing challenges. Rick and Pam differed in vacation plans. He wanted to go to places where he could deep-sea fish while she wanted a location to rummage for early American antiques. In each of these marriages, the couples have sincere differences and problems to solve. The wife in each of these marriages needs to bring to her marriage a commitment toward problem solving. She needs to have an attitude toward problem solving that can help her remain married successfully. I call this attitude, "the promise."

The promise is part of commitment in being married successfully. It represents an effective attitude toward marital problem solving. The promise applies equally to wives and husbands, but how it applies to you as a wife is focused on here.

This is the promise: "**I promise to do everything within my power to solve whatever problems come between us before I allow myself to even think about divorce.**" This means you don't get frustrated over a disagreement with your spouse and move prematurely in your mind to thoughts of divorce. It means you commit yourself to the exploration of every idea or approach possible to solve any problem in your marriage. Not only does the Promise bring out your creativity and flexibility, it brings forth your good will, too. Committing yourself to the Promise in the way you choose to be married can be a very powerful and directive force in your marriage.

If you bring the Promise to a marital problem, three possible outcomes will occur. There will be (1) problem solving, (2) problem acceptance, or (3) the identification of a marital condition that had not previously been known.

What follows is a set of three real-life scenarios: The first is a description of Sally and Gary's marital difference. It illustrates the problem-solving nature of the Promise. Next, Darcy and Bob's situation shows how applying the Promise can help with acceptance of a problem that is not going to be solved. And, finally, how applying the Promise can lead to the discovery of a condition and an understandable divorce, is shown in the marriage of Bill and Karen.

SALLY AND GARY

Sally and Gary had been married five years and had two young children. Christmas time was approaching. Sally wanted to organize Christmas between their respective families the same way this year as they had in the past five years. Gary wanted to change it. In the past, they had gone to his parents for Christmas eve and to her parents for Christmas day. This required a 60-mile drive in winter weather. Gary had tired of disrupting his and Sally's family in order to accommodate the tradition of going to their parents' homes for the holiday. He wanted to create a family tradition at home with his wife and kids, and to invite their parents to celebrate it with them. Sally worried this change would upset her parents. Gary was not insensitive to Sally's concerns. He thought his parents would be okay about it. They talked it over. They both listened and tried to understand each other. Sally agreed it would be nice to start their own tradition and that it would be better for the kids to be at home. They each agreed to call their parents and ask about changing Christmas plans. This was hard for Sally but she agreed to give it her best effort. They agreed that if either set of parents was upset with the idea, they would go along with the standard tradition this year, but would talk to their parents more throughout the year, so that it will be accepted that Christmas tradition will shift to Sally and Gary's house next year. They called their parents. Much to the relief of Sally and Gary, both sets of parents were delighted—they thought it would be great to shift the tradition to Sally and Gary's home. The problem was solved.

Sally and Gary had a problem. They applied their best thinking and energy, not to mention good will toward one another, and their efforts worked.

Sally (and Gary) illustrates the value of commitment to the Promise as an approach to problem solving. She did her best, stuck with it, challenged previously held positions, worked together, and solved a problem. Everybody who is married does this—has a problem, puts honest effort into it, and solves it. Problem resolution feels good and the marriage goes on. But, what do you do when you have a problem, do everything you can to solve it, and it doesn't get resolved?

THE MARRIED WOMAN

DARCY AND BOB

No matter to whom you are married to, you and your husband will have problems that you will *not solve*. Committing yourself to the Promise will help you realize the difference between a problem that could lead to divorce, and a problem of acceptance. Here is how Darcy and Bob applied the Promise to a difficult problem.

I remember Darcy talking to me about her difficulties with her husband's hobby. Bob was heavily involved in sailboat racing. He raced Wednesday and Sundays in the summer. In the winter he raced on Sundays, only. On Saturdays, though, he was down at the marina getting his boat ready for racing. He had a crew who also helped him, and toward whom Bob felt a commitment to keep his boat in top shape. It seemed to Darcy that Bob's racing went on all year long. At the beginning of the marriage, when they both had a lot of free time, Bob's racing schedule felt okay to Darcy. She even joined in it at times. Then the children were born. Darcy felt fine doing a lot of activities with the kids, and at times she would take them to visit Bob at his boat. When the children got a little older, Bob hoped they would get involved in racing, but that didn't happen. Occasionally, the whole family would enjoy a pleasure cruise, but for the most part, Bob's boat was made for racing and it was too cramped for the family.

By the time the children were in elementary school and Darcy had gone back to work at an accounting firm, the family dynamics had changed so much that it no longer felt right to Darcy for Bob to be gone so much. The years when it seemed that he had his boat, and she had her kids were over as far as she was concerned. She wanted him to spend more time with her and with the children.

Darcy did everything she could to get Bob to spend more time with the family, and less time with his boat. Bob listened to her, and he wasn't unsympathetic about her concerns. Bob tended to be a mellow person, rarely becoming angry or belligerent, so he generally made statements that sounded like he might try something different, but nothing changed. Darcy read a book about negotiating so that both husband and wife could get to "yes." This looked hopeful to her at first. She followed the book's guidelines and proposed a trade. She and the kids would help him with his boat on Saturdays if he would give up Wednesday evening racing. Bob agreed to give it a try. The agreement seemed to be working quite well, until a member of Bob's racing crew told him he was looking to join another crew that raced more often. Bob told Darcy he had to race one or two Wednesday nights to keep his crew from "jumping ship." The Wednesdays went by and the agreement slipped away.

By then Darcy was pretty frustrated. She suggested they try counseling to solve the problem. Bob, said, "no way. If we have a problem, we can solve it on our own." Bob said he would go back to their negotiated agreement about no Wednesday night racing. This lasted only one racing season, and the next season Bob was back into full scale racing on Wednesday nights. It was then Darcy knew she had done everything possible to solve the sailing/marriage problem.

There was nothing more Darcy could do. She had exhausted all solutions that fell under her control. She wished Bob would get counseling with her, but he refused. No solution seemed possible. I had the following conversation with Darcy about her situation.

"That's an interesting story," I said. "You are a very determined woman. I admire your commitment. You thought of a lot of alternatives. You did everything possible to solve the problem. It must be very frustrating, but I can't think of anything you could have done differently. Can you?"

"No," she said, resignedly, "I've tried and done everything I can think of."

"Did you ever get into withholding affection or attention in order to get Bob to change? I've known some spouses who have tried that."

"No," she said. "I wouldn't want him to do that to me if he didn't get his way, and I wouldn't do it either."

"Well, I'm glad you didn't. I don't recommend emotional bribery. It doesn't really work in marriages, and usually makes things worse."

"Can I ask you a question, Darcy?" She nodded in agreement.

"Darcy, do you want to be married to Bob? Has divorce ever entered your mind as you have been attempting to solve this problem?"

"You know," she said, "I've felt really frustrated and hurt at times, but I've never thought I should get a divorce. I've felt like strangling him a few times, but not divorce! I'm still frustrated, and I still believe he should spend more time with us, the kids and me. I think he's missing out on something really important in life. But, I'm not in charge of that for him. I've concluded that I just have to accept things the way they are. I still want to be married to Bob. I love him, and there is a lot of good in our marriage. It's not just about the time he spends with his racing. If the day comes that he spends less time with his boat, I'll be glad about it, but I've decided that for me to be happy, I have to turn attention to the things that I enjoy, and that the kids are involved in."

"So, you are choosing to be married to Bob even though you know he has no plans to significantly lessen his time with his hobby. I like what you've sorted out. You identified a problem in your marriage, did everything you realistically could to solve it, and have not let yourself be sidetracked into thinking about divorce. You accepted that you are making a rational choice for yourself. You've done something that is hard for all of us—you've accepted that sometimes things won't change."

"Yes, I guess that's what I did. But, I didn't know it would be so hard. When you get married, you think all the fantasies in your head about being married will begin to happen for real. Mostly, they don't, but that doesn't mean you get a divorce. I'm not going to take it out on Bob. He's not making me stay married. That's my decision. There's a lot good in our marriage, and I'm going to focus on that."

Darcy showed tremendous commitment to the Promise in the way she handled her situation with Bob. She identified a problem in her marriage, did everything she could think of to solve it, found that Bob wasn't really going to change and even that he wasn't interested in trying to solve this difference. So Darcy accepted that the problem was not going to get solved. Then she centered herself in her choice to be married. This enabled her to accept Bob's sailboat racing. Bob, (the husband) wasn't making Darcy (the wife) be married to him (the sail boat racer), it was her choice. Overall, Darcy felt her choice was a good one. By accepting what was not going to change, she was able to focus on the good in her marriage and not develop a grudge about Bob's racing.

It's easy to be judgmental of Bob. I would prefer him to spend less time with his boat and more time with his wife and kids. Most people who hear Darcy's story agree. But, Bob has a right to make his own choices, and Darcy has the right to choose what to accept, and to whom she'll be married. Not all of Darcy's preferences, not Bob's, not yours, will get met in marriage. As human beings we are too different for such sameness to occur.

Not all problems in marriage get solved, but that doesn't necessarily mean divorce should occur. It means acceptance that the situation will not change and that no one makes you be married but you. Commitment to the Promise allows you to go on with marriage and accept those aspects of marriage you do not like but over which you will not get a divorce. When you accept differences in your marriage you continue being married, as Darcy did, but you no longer blame your spouse because the problem didn't get solved. If you did all you could to solve the problem, and, despite the absence of a solution, you remain married, you are choosing to accept the difference and continue being married.

KAREN AND BILL

Remember previously, I explained that your participation in your marriage has conditions. I illustrated several conditions typically expressed by spouses such as unremitting affairs and abuse. While it is possible at any time in your marriage to identify infidelity and physical harm as fairly obvious conditions for your marital choice, how might one discover conditions as you go along? Some conditions you know in advance, while others may emerge later in your marriage. How do you tell the difference between a seeming condition and a real one? How do you prevent yourself from treating a non-condition as a condition and ending your marriage unnecessarily? Commitment to the Promise can help you sort out real from pseudo-conditions and allow you to feel assured that you are either accepting a difference or identifying a condition for continuing in your marriage.

Let's say you have a problem in your marriage. You do everything in your power to solve it, and the problem does not get solved. At that point you have the option to decide, as Darcy did, to accept the problem and go on with your marriage, thereby acknowledging that the problem is not a condition. Or, you could decide that you no longer choose to be married because the problem is not a difference you can just accept, but a condition with which you will not live. In other words, the problem is either something you accept or it is a condition, and therefore unacceptable, and you get a divorce. If no conditions emerge in your marriage, you stay married because problems are either solved or accepted as differences. Here is the story of how Karen discovered a problem in her marriage, did everything in her power to solve it, concluded it would never change, considered it impossible to remain married, and got a divorce. Karen was strongly committed to the Promise. If you were

Karen, what would you have done?

When I first met Karen she was deeply in love with her husband, Bill. She felt completely committed to the marriage, and couldn't even imagine being married to anyone else. She found Bill to be attentive, sensitive, and loving. Bill's sense of humor was especially endearing to Karen, and she loved that he could easily make her laugh. They rarely argued, and when they did have a disagreement, they would make up quickly. Karen thought her marriage to Bill was wonderful and, compared to other marriages she knew about, almost too good to be true.

Karen had a college degree, and before their child was born, she had worked as an escrow officer. They planned to have one more child, and then Karen would return to work. While Bill had not gone to college, his job as manager of a local construction company in Seattle provided enough money for them to live comfortably. Karen had a lifelong relationship with God and attended church regularly, while Bill believed in God but didn't feel attending church was important. Karen had adjusted to this difference and didn't mind going to church on her own. Karen was in a wonderful groove as a wife, and she felt confident in her marriage—until one day she was shocked out of her marital bliss. What happened that shook Karen to the very foundation of her marital commitment?

As she often did, Karen took the baby to spend the day visiting her mother some 60 miles away. Karen arrived only to find her mother feeling ill, and they both decided that they should not expose the baby to whatever "bug" her mother might have. Karen wished her mother well, turned around and drove home again. She arrived home, went inside quietly so as not to wake her sleeping infant, and laying the baby into her crib, Karen tiptoed down to her bedroom, where she was startled to find Bill—looking shocked and shamefaced—dressed head to foot in women's clothing! Karen was astonished. She couldn't believe her eyes.

Confusing as the scene was, she maintained her composure, thinking against all hope that it was a joke. Bill didn't look amused. He appeared scared and guilty. He asked her to give him a little time, to wait in the living room, and he would be out in a few minutes. The minutes seemed like an eternity as Karen waited for her husband. Questions ran through her mind, her hands shook, and she began to cry.

When Bill came into the living room, Karen was relieved to see that he looked like himself again. Bill came up to Karen to hug her, but she pushed him away. There was a long silence and then Bill began to talk. He explained to her that he had dressed in women's clothing since his teenage years, and that he used it as a way to excite himself sexually. He didn't want to tell her about it when they were engaged because he was afraid she wouldn't marry him. He thought of telling her a hundred times but didn't because he knew that she would be shocked, and might even leave him. Bill admitted that he hoped he could hide this from her forever, and that their marriage would always be as good as it had been up until that moment of discovery. Karen's tears turned to anger and dismay. Why hadn't he told her? What was wrong with him? What could be done about it? She said, in a voice just above a whisper, that she thought he was "not right." Bill began to cry, too. He said he was sorry, and that he would stop. It would never happen again. He looked so pitiful and remorseful, Karen's caring heart went out to him. She believed him, he would stop, everything would be okay. They held each other until the tears stopped. Bill thanked Karen for believing in him, and they made up.

After this, there were times of uneasiness, but when several months had gone by and everything seemed normal again, Karen was delighted to learn that she was pregnant with their second child. She was feeling good and confident about her marriage again. The incident was in the past, and with the anticipated birth of her baby, it felt finished.

Bill remained an attentive husband, especially through the birth of their new baby. Then one day, when the baby was two months old, Karen needed some papers for completing their tax forms. She was in a hurry to get everything gathered up while the children were napping, which led her to dash out of the house to look in Bill's work truck to see if some of the missing receipts were in there. As she rummaged through his things, she found a backpack filled with women's clothing. Flabbergasted and heartsick, she couldn't decide what to do. By then she also felt guilty for having gone to his truck—she had trusted Bill, and this made her feel as if she had been snooping. With a heavy heart, she dragged the pack into the house, passing Bill in the kitchen. The instant he saw the backpack, guilt was obvious in his look. With tears in her eyes, Karen said to him, "How could you do to this to me?"

So, once again, Karen sat down to talk it out with Bill. She expressed her feelings that this could not continue. Bill agreed to go to counseling at Karen's insistence, and a strained truce descended upon their marriage. To the rest of the world, their marriage looked just about like it always had, but nothing felt the same to Karen.

After a few weeks, Bill had done nothing about making an appointment to see someone for counseling, so Karen brought it up again. By then, however, Bill said he no longer felt that counseling would be necessary, and he had decided to handle it himself. At that point, he finally asked Karen to try to accept him wearing women's clothing. "I'm not hurting anyone with it—it's, it's just what I do!" he said. "Why can't you just leave it alone?"

Karen was so hurt by this that she started to cry. She couldn't understand why Bill had hidden this from her, why he had told her he would stop it, and even more, how he could expect her to accept his behavior. "I wasn't brought up this way. It's just wrong. You shouldn't be doing it, that's all I know. There is something wrong with you. You have to get help. I'll go with you if that will make it easier. I'll even make the appointment, but you have to get help."

When Bill agreed again to counseling, Karen called around to find an appointment with a psychologist. This is how I got to know Karen and Bill. We talked on the phone, and made an appointment to help them explore their options.

In their weekly sessions, I helped Karen and Bill communicate more clearly. Bill talked about his background, and how he developed his cross-dressing behaviors. Karen hadn't heard any of this before, so she listened intently to him. She learned it has nothing to do with wanting to be a woman, or being gay. She began to understand more about cross-dressing, and how important this had been in Bill's life. I gave them literature to read about the subject, which helped Karen talk about her beliefs, and the values that she held concerning cross-dressing.

I asked them to explore options for finding a solution to this problem that had arisen in their marriage. Karen believed that Bill was sick and should seek help for getting rid of this part of himself, while Bill believed that Karen should lighten up about the whole matter. He suggested that she learn to accept it, and let it be part of their mutual sex life. Karen was shocked by this proposal but was willing to consider it for the sake of their children and life together.

Karen was living up to the Promise by continuing to be married to Bill, and by remaining open to ways of solving this problem. At this stage, she was neither thinking nor talking about divorce. She wanted to find a way to be married to Bill. She even agreed to try what Bill suggested about letting this become part of their sex life together. Karen was absolutely committed to solving the problem, if possible. Finally, she said that she would try to accept Bill's cross-dressing. Bill was thrilled and hopeful by her openness. Karen was fearful and less than confident about her choice, but willing for the sake of her marriage to see it through.

Karen and Bill decided to take it slowly at home. It seemed as though they were both walking on eggshells, neither one wanting to upset the other, or make a move that would cause their fragile agreement to fall apart. But one night, not too long after Karen's agreement, Bill became amorous with her. Karen's anxiety level went up but she kept in mind what she was hoping to gain. "Just a minute, I'll be right back," Bill said to her.

As Karen waited in the semi-darkness of their bedroom, she had a talk with herself about commitment, and making adjustments, and how much she had always loved Bill. When Bill reentered the bedroom, Karen could see in the dim lighting that he was cross-dressed in women's underclothes and makeup. She closed her eyes and attempted to see Bill in the same way that she had always visualized him. In their lovemaking, he was sensitive and tender with her. He was very excited in his attempts to please her. She could feel the garter belt, the nylons, and the lingerie. She could taste the make-up and lipstick as he kissed her. It was like making love to someone else entirely. Karen felt repulsed.

Thoughts raced through Karen's mind: How could Bill do this to me? What have I agreed to? I can't do this! She really didn't know what in the world she would do. Everything felt all wrong to her.

For the rest of the week, waiting for their next session, an eerie kind of peace settled into Karen and Bill's home. Bill was relieved that they had experienced their first romantic episode under the new agreement. He took this to mean that Karen was adjusting, and that everything was going to work out after all. "Now I can bring my true sexual feelings into our marriage," he told me later.

Karen was much more troubled than she could let on to Bill. She knew that she could not do it again. She feared that Bill would bring it up again before their next session. She knew that Bill had been more excited about making love with her than he ever had in the past, and she felt repulsed by that. Karen felt profoundly sad and disappointed.

In our next session, I helped them describe their thoughts and feelings about having engaged in sex while including Bill's cross-dressing. It became clear immediately that there was a huge difference in their interpretation of their sexual exchange. Karen shuddered as she spoke of her revulsion, and Bill talked about how he thought it had been great. A profound sadness overcame Karen as she began to realize that Bill was not the man that she had fallen in love with.

At home, Karen went back to urging Bill to get help, and he did agree to think about it. But at the same time, he withdrew from Karen and began sleeping in another room. They continued to have interactions about the children, and moved into an almost exclusively mom-and-dad mode of relating to one another. They weren't connecting in the ways that they always had, and when it came time for their next therapy session, Bill said he wasn't going to go.

Karen began seeing me on her own at that point, with the idea that she didn't yet know where she wanted her life to go from there. Karen had told me that she hadn't ever been able to conceive of herself being married to anyone other than Bill. Now, she reported she couldn't imagine ever putting herself through another night like the last time she and Bill had sex together. And yet, when she told me that Bill was becoming more withdrawn and depressed, she said that it broke her heart to see him hurting so much. He was no longer willing to come to see me for therapy, and had refused to see anyone else either. She wanted to be married to Bill, and was willing to do almost anything to see that happen. I admired her courage in the face of this challenge to her marital commitment. She talked about hopes, and fears, and as she talked I could almost see the words and ideas swirl around in her mind—trying to solidify into a plan she could live with.

Karen did want to be married to Bill. But could she live with his cross-dressing? Could she really LIVE with it? She knew she couldn't accept it. She had ideas about morality that conflicted with her desire to continue being married to Bill. On the one hand, she wanted to be married to Bill, and on the other she had to remain true to her moral values. A dilemma is a dilemma because there can be more than one correct answer to it. Another woman might discover that her husband is a cross-dresser and, after a bit of time adjusting to it, find that it is an acceptable situation. That would be one way to answer the problem of cross-dressing in a marriage. But for Karen, that was simply not possible. Yet she struggled with her own feelings because she knew that it was (at least theoretically) possible for someone to accept this situation and go on being married. As the sessions progressed, Karen began to find acceptance of another kind.

Karen came to recognize that cross-dressing is a condition that she is unwilling to ignore, or accept, or adjust to. She could not feel faithful to her own moral values, and her sense of who she is, if she were to try to be married to someone who cross-dresses. She also recognized that it might be in Bill's sense of self to cross-dress, and that was his right.

With every bit of strength and resolve she could pull together, Karen gave it one more try to see if Bill would get help. If not, she knew her marriage was over. She went home and told Bill that she could not be married to someone who wears female clothing and does not get help to stop it. "I really believe you have the right to do what you want, so I'm not telling you what to do. I'm just trying to explain where I'm coming from. I've come to realize that you have a right to cross-dress. With someone else it might be okay. I guess we are both pretty stuck in our ways. I know in my heart that I can't be married to someone who cross-dresses. I just can't. I'm truly sorry—I didn't want it to turn out this way, but I just can't. I wish you would get help with it."

Bill said, "I'm sorry, too, Karen," and then he walked away. Karen's heart sank. She knew at that point that she had done everything she could, explored every option, thought of every approach within her moral range. She knew Bill was going to continue to cross-dress, and she knew that there was nothing she could do about it. She knew that her feelings wouldn't change—it was not a moral possibility for her to accept it. What had been unthinkable to her before had become a reality. She would have to get a divorce.

After several months, Karen and Bill's divorce was final, and Karen had begun to create a new life for herself and her children. Bill continued to be a good father after the divorce, just as he had been before. Karen assumed that Bill continued his practice of cross-dressing, but it was not something that they talked about when the children were picked up or dropped off. She had no fears that Bill would introduce cross-dressing to the kids. He cross-dressed but he was a mature adult man and a loving father. She felt confident about this. In her heart, Karen hoped for good things in life for Bill. She hoped he would find someone with whom he could share himself fully. If not, she hoped that one day he would decide to get some help with his cross-dressing, so that he could live happily without it. She deeply regretted that her marriage with Bill had not worked out, but she was very clear about herself and that she had done what was right for her.

Karen accepted responsibility for herself as an adult. She recognized her obligation to make moral choices for herself, and she accepted this burden. Doing what was right for her was hard but necessary for her to live with herself. By recognizing all this, Karen was able to feel confident and proud of herself despite the loss of her marriage. She could clearly see how, at every step of her marital process, she had remained true to her commitment to the Promise. This gave her much comfort at those times when she felt really heartbroken, or guilty, about having "a failed marriage." She could honestly say to herself that her marriage had failed, but that as a wife she had not.

It would never have occurred to Karen to ask herself, when she first began dating as a teenager and young adult, "I wonder whether I would be okay married to a person who cross-dresses?" Karen simply didn't think about this as a possibility, and there never came a time until that fateful day when she returned home unexpectedly, that Karen considered she would be married to a man who cross-dressed for sexual pleasure. But when she discovered that her husband wore women's clothing, she had to confront her own reaction to cross-dressing. And in confronting her own responses she learned that she had a condition for being married. She could not be married to a man who cross-dressed and planned to continue doing it. It would have been utterly impossible for Karen to spend time wondering whether she could be married to someone who cross-dresses before she learned this new information about her husband. But it would have been equally impossible for her to continue being married to him after recognizing that it was a condition for her being married or not to anyone.

The stories of Sally and Darcy and Karen offer different perspectives on the Promise. In their marriage, each of these wives had love and commitment going for them. Each had a turning point—one in which there was a problem requiring their attention—and each wife put the Promise into action. Sally's problem was relatively easy: She and Gary both were actively involved in the solution, and their parents were agreeable to the changes they proposed, so that everyone was happy in the end.

Darcy and Bob exemplify how the enactment of the Promise can lead to acceptance of a problem, and it is important to note that this problem really came down to Darcy's decision to accept Bob's choices. Bob didn't participate in any real way in creating or finding a solution, and he wasn't deeply concerned about continuing to search for ways to "compromise." Darcy accepted the problem without mutual resolution because of the Promise that states, "I will do everything within my power...." When Darcy had "done everything" she also recognized that her marriage was valuable on many levels. Since Darcy had done everything possible to obtain resolution to the problem, and she discovered it was not a condition for whether she would remain married or not, she did the rational thing and accepted the problem. All wives do this in their marriages—have a problem, try to solve it, can't, accept things as they are—and remain married. If you can't solve it but you are not going to get a divorce over it, then accept it and go on with your marriage. Darcy saw the Promise through and continued her marriage past the problem.

Karen and Bill's marriage ended when Karen found a problem that could not be solved, and could not be accepted. Bill's preference for cross-dressing was a condition for whether she would be married or not. At the conclusion of their marriage, Bill was sad, and Karen was very hurt and disappointed, but Karen knew she had given it her best effort. The Promise gives you that assurance, even if you get a divorce. For most spouses, knowing they have tried their best reduces feelings of guilt, and provides some comfort of the sorrow that they naturally feel.

It is also important to know that you are much more likely to continue being married than to get a divorce, if you understand and commit yourself to the Promise in your marriage. Adults have conditions that are rational and reasonable for whether it makes sense to remain married. And they are extremely capable of solving problems if they put their best effort forward. Thus, the Promise leads to strong problem solving, and a rational, adult married life. Commitment to the Promise means that you are much more likely to solve problems or accept them, than you are to discover conditions that prevent you from continuing in your marriage. In my 25 years of working with couples, I have seen spouses solve, or find ways of living with, almost every conceivable problem. Putting your very best effort into solving a problem, accepting problems that cannot be solved, or recognizing a condition for what it is, are all reasonable and rational marital actions. Usually when commitment is framed around a rational idea such as the Promise better marital results are attained.

ADOPTING THE PROMISE

As we go along, I will ask you to integrate important ideas and beliefs toward being married successfully into your sense of yourself as a married woman. This is the same as making the orientation part of your color as a wife. This internalization process is important if you are to survive and succeed in marriage. There are two ways you can integrate the promise into your marriage. One is about you and your husband, and the other is primarily about you.

First, you can go to your husband and tell him that you've just read about a "promise-centered" approach to commitment in marriage, and you want to tell him about it. Explain it, or have him read the section on "the promise" for himself. Tell him you want to commit yourself to this ideal, and you want him to know it. Don't tell him he should also commit himself—this is about you not about him. Be sure to mention that you know this will not prevent you from having any problems in your marriage, because—as we know—problems are part of the marital territory. Just let him know that you want to take this "promise-centered" approach rather than a problem-centered approach to your marriage.

You can also ask him if he would like to join you in making a commitment to the Promise in his approach to being married to you. He might like to think about it, or even read some of this book. Make the Promise to yourself, and then be open to talking about it with him. Let him lead himself as he explores his own decision. Just remember that what he decides for himself is not under your control, but what you decide to do for yourself is squarely under your direction.

The second way that you can integrate the Promise into your sense of commitment is to focus solely on yourself and devise some kind of ceremony to indicate that you've come to a new understanding, or agreement with yourself (or with your husband if he has joined you on this)—a new state of awareness called the "Promise." You'll remember that when you were going through whatever type of marriage ceremony you had, that it was a type of turning point. The whole idea of doing a Promise ceremony is to internalize your commitment into your marital sense of self. Repeat the Promise to yourself like a mantra, say it to your God, burn some incense, or tell it to a special spot in the woods or along the seashore. Do whatever you have to do to connect this new Promise to the deepest part of your marital belief and commitment. By internalizing the Promise it becomes part of your thinking and acting; part of you—part of your color. Whether you tell your husband or keep it to yourself, make the Promise the foundation for the way you approach problems in your commitment as a wife from now on. It is a promise-centered attitude that can be of immense help in having a successful, adult marriage.

MARRIAGE MAKEOVER
STEP FIVE

Non-Iffy Love

*How to connect loving him
to your choice to be married
and not his behavior.*

WHEN I INTERVIEW COUPLES, I always ask each spouse if he or she has feelings of love for the other, even though feelings have been hurt and problems have occurred in their marriage. If feelings of love are present, I believe any problem other than a condition can be solved and the marriage improved. If love is absent, I find spouses unable to muster the motivation to work out their problems. They have no emotional reason to accommodate and adjust. Without love, I see marriages end. With love, I see marriages continue. I believe that love is the soul of a marriage. But, how should you love in order for fulfillment to find itself into your heart and into your marriage? Is there a way of loving that brings the best of you into the marriage?

The inability to solve problems and be married successfully is heartbreaking because it prevents you from feeling good about your experience of love. That is the price spouses ultimately pay in a dysfunctional marriage. Love becomes a basis for hurt rather than fulfillment. Repairing your marriage enables you to get on with filling your heart with the love you feel as a married woman.

Since love is essential to marriage, you should commit yourself to the best kind of loving possible. You should know how to love so that the greatest possible fulfillment can occur for you in your choice to be married. What kind of love is this? It is non-iffy loving—it is offering your love to your husband without contingencies. It is loving not with your eyes but with your heart.

Elect to love your husband based on your decision to be married. You know you don't want a loveless marriage, so if you've decided you want to continue being married to this man, decide also to love him, to maintain affection for him no matter what he may do. Loving him like this is loving without ifs. It is loving him even though he gets old, develops a big belly, complains too much, ignores you and hurts your feelings, criticizes you unjustly, gets depressed, becomes disfigured from an accident, acquires a disabling illness, drinks too much, or gets fired. It is loving him because you are choosing to be married to him, not because of the way he acts. It is connecting your love for your husband to your choice to be married to him and not to his behavior. Don't let yourself fall into contingent loving—loving him because he says the right things, acts in the right ways, believes in the right things (according to you). Make your love free and without ifs—he doesn't have to do anything to earn it nor can he do anything to lessen it. You are in charge of loving him and your love is connected only to your choice to be married to him.

Because you may be in a difficult marriage and are experiencing hurt and anger, you may not feel at present like loving this way. You may feel like saying, "Yeah, right. I should love him no matter what, but look at the way he has been treating me. He doesn't deserve this kind of love." If these contingent feelings of love are your starting place, okay. But set your sights on connecting your love to your choice to be married to him, and not to his behavior. Decide to put loving him into the color of your wife sphere where it belongs and where you are in charge of it. Begin to turn yourself toward this kind of loving. Your love will get tested many times in your marriage. You will have many opportunities to locate your love in you and not in the ways he is behaving. Your present starting place represents an opportunity of the moment. Make non-iffy loving your goal. The challenges we present ourselves often turn out to be the reality of who we become. Resolve to become a wife who locates love in herself and extends it to her husband without ifs.

You are an adult woman and no one can make you be married but you. As long as you choose to be married it will make sense to go about being married in such a way that it can work best for you. Loving your husband should be connected to your choice to be married, only. Since marriage is about love and its fulfillment, and you are choosing to be married, love in a way that makes for the greatest possible fulfillment. Develop a love that is not determined by anything beyond the nature of your loving and your choice to be married to him. The only time to consider not loving him is if you stop being married to him.

MARRIAGE MAKEOVER

STEP SIX

Being Faithful

Your Fidelity is Your responsibility.

OVER THE YEARS I have seen spouses try all sorts of sexual arrangements in marriages. Some have tried open marriage, a concept and practice promoted in the late sixties as a form of being married that included sex with other partners. Other marital participants have shared with me their attempt to accommodate a bisexual spouse's interest in sex with his or her marital partner and sex with a same sex partner outside the marriage. I have known spouses who have lived with their marital partner and included in the household another love partner with all three sharing sex with one another. Some couples have tried maintaining the appearance of monogamy while agreeing that one spouse, usually the man, could have a mistress as long as it is kept secret from family and society. Other couples have pretended a vow of fidelity while engaging secretly in one or more affairs on the side during the course of the marriage. Secret affairs constitute the "standard" idea of an affair in American culture. Surveys estimate that from 20% to 40% of women and 30% to 60% of men have this kind of affair.

One of the fundamental questions all spouses must address is whether to be faithful in their marriage. Almost all spouses promise to be faithful but not all spouses do it. How about you? Should you be faithful? If your think you should, how best do you do it?

There are two parts to faithfulness, first, deciding to be faithful, and second, knowing how to do it. If you decide on fidelity, you must know how to do it—how to maintain your commitment of fidelity in all situations, over all ages, throughout your marital life.

While couples have revealed to me different models of sharing sex with non-spouse partners, I have never seen any of them work. I have seen some of these marriages endure, however, I have never witnessed any of the arrangement described above result in marital fulfillment. I have concluded that you can be married and have other sex partners, but you cannot be married and feel good about yourself and your marriage if you do. I think being faithful is the way to be married. Why? There are two answers, one that lies in the construct of marriage in our culture, and the other in the pragmatics of trust in marital expectations.

In the current American culture, marriage is primarily about love and its fulfillment. Loving someone in our culture means arranging affection, sex, intimacy and romance so that these sharings enhance your love. In our culture, the imperative is to pursue satisfaction and fulfillment with one partner. Our culture "says," marriage works best when spouses have sex and intimacy with each other, only. Our culture expects marriage to be the vehicle of greatest hope for this to occur. If you want and desire a successful marriage today in American culture, then it is important to maintain monogamy.

Fidelity in marriage is a cultural imperative. While sexual activity outside the marriage occurs, it is generally frowned upon and considered unacceptable and even foolish in our society. The expectation when you marry is that you will contain intimacy and sexual sharing within your marriage exclusively. To engage in infidelity is to break a cultural norm. Breaking the rules of one's culture creates a level of psychological discomfort that runs counter to satisfaction and fulfillment. The pursuit of marital fulfillment is best accomplished within the norms of one's culture. Managing marital activity within, and consistent with, cultural expectations helps one feel peace and contentment. Attempting to arrange marital activity outside of cultural norms produces disenchantment and failure. Fidelity in marriage is a cultural norm. Just as driving down the right side of the road is safe and comfortable in America, so too, is fidelity.

Fidelity is also a pragmatic imperative. Most marriages include a promise to remain faithful. Faithfulness is part of commitment: "I will share my intimacy and sexuality with you only." Sometimes this injunction is stated and other times it is assumed. Nonetheless, the expectation of fidelity is clearly part of being married in America.

INFIDELITY

Given the cultural and pragmatic imperative for fidelity in American marriages, it is helpful to know what constitutes fidelity and infidelity so as to guide yourself successfully in marriage.

Infidelity is being emotionally intimate and/or sexual with someone other than your husband in the context of having pledged faithfulness. It is more than having sex/intercourse with another man. It is sharing your closeness and intimacy—your emotional and/or physical vulnerabilities—with him. Because of the marital pledge to be faithful, unfaithfulness is an act of betrayal. Through this act of betrayal you bring dishonesty, lack of dependability, lack of reliability, and untrust-worthiness into the marriage. Being a wife who brings these behaviors into the marriage makes it impossible to feel good about yourself as a wife, and impossible to feel fulfillment of love in your marriage. The fulfillment of love requires emotional trust, a willingness to be open and vulnerable. Being untrue to your promises and unfaithful in your marriage creates mountains of distrust. How can you lie, sneak, plot and betray, all behaviors required to have an affair, and expect to feel good about yourself as a wife or have a marriage you regard as successful? It isn't possible.

FIDELITY

Being faithful means you draw the emotional and sexual line between you and men other than your husband. Just because you are married and have a ring on your finger, does not mean men will not come on to you and that you will not have situations where emotional involvement with another man can occur. When men flirt with women, they are trying to find out where you will draw the sexual line. When you stand your ground, men back off. When you don't, men continue to flirt until you are forced to draw your line. In most cases, if you draw the line with yourself naked and in bed with another man, that is where the line will reside. Most men put women in charge of where the line will be drawn. I wish they didn't. I wish men would draw the line where it is good for them and for their own life goals to draw it. Some men know how to do this. These are very centered and mature men. They are a joy to know and to be around. These men know how to be friends with women. Men who flirt and don't know how to draw their own lines, rely on women rather than themselves to maintain sexual boundaries. Of course, when you flirt with a man, you are also exploring where the two of you will draw the intimacy/sexuality line between you.

When a man flirts with you, you must draw the line where it is good for you to draw it and not where a man would like you to draw it. You must draw the line so that your life goals of a successful marriage can occur. I call this your wife sphere line. Here's an example of two wives, Jane who did a poor job of drawing her sphere line, and Peggy, who was tested but maintained her line exceedingly well.

Jane knew where the line was but felt compelled because of psychological insecurities to test it over and over again in her marriage. Her marriage eventually ended because of her flirtations.

Jane and Luke had been married two years. Jane was a beautiful woman, but insecure. Whenever she and Luke had an intense argument, Jane would put on her mini-skirt, say, "If that's the way you want it, see you later," and off to a bar she went. At the bar, men would flirt with her and come on to her and she would flirt back. She would get her pretty-woman-self-esteem-build-up and go home when the bar closed, alone. This pattern had gone on for a year-and-a-half when I saw them.

Luke was at his wit's end. He hated waiting at home for Jane to return. He thought she didn't screw around but only flirted, but he wasn't sure. He was close to ending his marriage with Jane. He said so in our first session. When Luke said he was considering divorce, Jane's insecurities were further aroused and before this issue could be effectively addressed in our sessions, she went too far. Jane and Luke had one of their usual fights, she left as she had on many occasions, but this time she didn't come home. She apparently drank too much, became intrigued with a guy whom she found extremely attractive, went to his apartment and to bed with him. This was the end for Luke. He knew he could not have the marriage he wanted with Jane and he felt she had little desire to change her pattern of behavior. He got a divorce. Luke told me later that Jane had moved in with the guy she met at the bar that night, stayed with him for several months and then they broke up. He has not heard much about her since.

Jane had trouble drawing the line between herself and other men. Anytime she felt upset, she used her looks to get guys to flirt with her. She relied on the flirting game to build up her self-esteem. It didn't work. Jane's behavior of going to bars alone, flirting, staying out late, and finally, having an affair brought problems of distrust, dishonesty, disloyalty, immaturity and lack of commitment into the marriage. Ironically,

BEING FAITHFUL

the very behaviors she hoped would boost her self-esteem—flirting—defeated her hopes for long term security. Jane did not know how to draw the marital sphere line between her and other men and it led to the end of her marriage. If Jane had stayed in marital therapy a little longer, these issues could have been addressed. Hopefully, by confronting her insecurities, learning how to manage her wife sphere, and taking responsibility for where she drew her wife sphere line, she would have saved her marriage.

Not all cases of drawing the wife sphere line are as dramatic as Jane's. Peggy had an incident in her marriage that severely tested where she would draw the line. Married 12 years to Chuck, she had never had a desire for intimacy with other men. She loved her husband and he loved her. They both knew how to love each other and how to protect their love from outside involvements.

One evening at home watching TV with Chuck, Peggy got a tragic call that her father had unexpectedly died of a heart attack. Peggy flew to Idaho Falls the next day to be with her mother and to bury her father while Chuck stayed home with the kids. At the funeral reception, she was greeted by her old high school boyfriend and first lover, Ron. He was recently divorced and lived close to Peggy's parents. Ron had known Peggy's father well and while they were dating in high school, he was almost part of the family. It was good to see Ron, and Peggy was able to express her feelings of grief with him. Peggy spent the afternoon walking in a nearby park with Ron and talking a lot about her dad, and high school times, and some about Ron's divorce. Just like in the old days, talk came easily to Peggy and Ron. Ron suggested they have dinner and Peggy agreed. They talked and talked over dinner and wine. On the way back to Peggy's house, Ron pulled over and brought the car to a stop under some overhanging tree branches. He reached over and took Peggy into his arms and said, "I just want to hold you." At first the hug felt good to Peggy, then something told her a line had been crossed and this wasn't a friendly, comforting hug, but an intimate and perhaps sexual hug. For an instant, with fatigue and grief unbalancing her hormones and emotions, she felt the urge to respond to Ron's hug, like she had in the old days when they had parked and she had had her first sexual experience with him. Then she caught herself and pulled back. She joked, "Boy, where did that come from?" Ron said it was no joke, that he had never forgotten her and wanted to see her again. Peggy told Ron that she wanted to just be friends, and that when she came out with Chuck and the kids she would like for him to meet them—maybe they could all hang out together. Ron said he wanted more than that; he wanted to see Peggy alone. He proposed flying her to a vacation spot and getting a room for them to meet. Peggy said that wasn't possible. "The only relationship we can have, Ron, is as friends. If you can't accept that, then no relationship is possible at all." Ron said he was sorry she felt that way. She asked him to drive her home. That was the last time Peggy saw Ron.

Peggy knew where to draw her marital sphere line with Ron. Ron confused friendship and intimacy. When he felt friendship with Peggy, he thought it meant sexual intimacy as well. His hug and verbal proposal for a liaison, was an exploration of where Peggy would draw her sexual line. Peggy was tempted by the closeness and her vulnerability and the ease of relating to Ron, to lose track of where her line was. She was tested, but she drew her line where it was good for her and her values as a wife to draw it. Peggy was able to exit her situation with Ron feeling bad that she could not have a friendship with him, but proud of herself as a wife and with the hope of fulfilling her marital love with Chuck intact.

Jane did a poor job of drawing her marital sphere line, while Peggy did it well. Jane's life is not working out well for her. Fulfilling her hopes for herself does not look bright. On the other hand, Peggy is on track.

BEING FAITHFUL

She knows how to draw the line within which her sphere as a wife exists and, consequently, is able to guide herself toward pride and fulfillment.

Just as Peggy did, it is your responsibility to maintain the boundary and integrity of your wife sphere line in your marriage. Knowing that you have a wife sphere boundary no matter where, when, or in what situation you find yourself enables you to guide yourself effectively. This means you consistently draw the boundary of your sphere between you and other men. You draw the line where it is possible for you to feel good about yourself as a wife and within which the parameters of hope and marital fulfillment exist. You do not draw the line where other men want to you draw it, or where flirting will momentarily make you feel attractive and desirable. Instead, you draw it so that your life can include a successful marital experience and so you can become fulfilled in your choice to be married. Learn to draw your line so that it works for you. It's not like you are being faithful because your husband wants you to— husbands can't make wives be faithful— but rather because you made a choice to be married and for your own purposes in life you want to make it work.

Fidelity is being intimate and sexual with your husband and no one else. It is abiding by the pledge in your marriage to remain faithful. It is being trustworthy, reliable, dependable and honest. Fidelity keeps the energy of your intimacy and sexuality within the parameters of your marriage. It allows for emotional vulnerability to exist. Fidelity helps you grant yourself pride and fulfillment as a wife. Commit yourself to being faithful. Put the idea firmly in your marital mind and maintain your marital boundaries no matter where and in what circumstance you find yourself. You are in charge of your wife sphere and its boundaries at work, on a train, plane, bus, at a conference, at a cafe, in a bar, at your high school reunion, out with the girls, or wherever you find yourself. Make fidelity part of your color as a wife.

MARRIAGE MAKEOVER

STEP SEVEN

Your Commitment Mission Statement

*How does a reasonable and
rational married woman
commit herself to being married?*

SENTIMENTS ABOUT AN ETERNAL LOVE and life together are nice, but they don't get the job done. As we have seen, real life commitment is about (1) the choice to be married, (2) rational and reasonable self-regard, (3) problem solving, (4) centered and non-iffy love, and (5) faithfulness. If you want success and fulfillment as a married woman, these are the things you must commit yourself to. Not necessarily earth-shaking ideas, but practical ones, that can make being married work well over time.

    Commitment is part of your mission as a married woman. There will be obstacles, there will be setbacks, and there will be moments of confusion as you travel through your marital life. Clearly knowing how to do commitment will help you make your journey successful. You will be required to be single minded and creative at the same time, as you figure out the maze of twists and turns of commitment. But, if you keep

YOUR COMMITMENT MISSION STATEMENT

your mission clearly in mind, you will prevail.

Here's the mission statement for a reasonable and rationally committed married woman:

> I am choosing to be a married woman; nobody can make me be married but me. I will do all that I can to make my choice successful. I have reasonable and rational conditions for whether I will be married to anyone. Conditions are not ultimatums. My conditions apply to my choice to be married, and not to my husband's actions. When a problem occurs in my marriage, I will do everything within my power to solve it. If a problem can be solved, great! If a problem cannot be solved and it is not a condition, I will learn to live with it. I will take charge of my love for my husband and will extend it to him without contingencies or ifs. I will be faithful, and I will maintain the integrity of my wife sphere line in all life situations.

PART FOUR: WORKING ON SUCCESS

MARRIAGE MAKEOVER

STEP EIGHT

Becoming an Action Valued Married Woman

How do you identify your guidance system
for being a married woman?
Here's how Cheryl did it.

HOW DO YOU GO ABOUT BEING A MARRIED WOMAN in the practical everyday activity of marriage so that fulfillment can occur? It is by knowing how to guide yourself in a value-centered way. Working on fulfillment can help you dig your way out of the despair of marital distress, and put into place a guidance system for being successfully married. This work requires that you develop a personal guidance system as a married woman no matter to whom you would be married. The values that make up your guidance system identify your philosophy for being a married woman. This type of knowing and being can make you a value-centered wife. By becoming value-centered, you can be a married woman who knows who she is and how she wants to be in all marital situations. It's what we will be calling *being on track*.

This next section is about identifying your action values—actions that reflect your best values as a married woman. When you act in ways that are consistent with your action values, you are on track. The better you get on track, stay on track, and get back on track when you get off, the more fulfillment you will experience as a married woman.

WHAT HAPPENED TO CHERYL'S MARRIAGE?

Remember Cheryl? I told you I would come back to her story and share with you how she became successfully married and increased her marital fulfillment. When I saw her, Cheryl had been married to Ed for five years. It was her second marriage. She had a child from her first marriage and another from her marriage with Ed. She was back to work as an elementary school teacher. Ed's business took a downturn and Ed took an emotional nosedive. He withdrew into his business worries and became emotionally unavailable to Cheryl. She got hurt and angry. She pleaded, yelled, and threatened to leave, in her frustration to get Ed to come out of his funk—but to no avail—he remained withdrawn and seclusive. Cheryl and Ed began sleeping in separate bedrooms. Ed refused to go to counseling. A robotic stalemate ensued with neither of them interacting much outside the children's needs. This was the state of Cheryl's marriage when she came to see me. She didn't want a divorce but she was feeling miserable and heartbroken in her marriage to Ed.

I first helped Cheryl sort through her feelings about commitment. She got clear that she was an adult woman choosing to be married, that her choice had conditions (but that one of her conditions was not Ed's present state of withdrawal); that she would do everything in her power to solve problems between her and Ed before even letting herself think about divorce; that she would try to love Ed without contingencies and connect her love only to her choice to be a wife and not to Ed's behavior; and that she would remain faithful. Cheryl struggled with some of the ideas of commitment. It was not easy to acknowledge her choice and especially her conditions—she had a tough time deciding that Ed's emotional abandonment of her was not a condition. Getting clear about loving him openly and without contingencies was also difficult because Cheryl felt that it was unfair for Ed to withdraw from her in the marriage. Cheryl wanted to react and judge and withhold her love—to connect her love to Ed's behavior. When she understood that centered and non-iffy love was the only way to love as an adult woman choosing to be married, Cheryl began to orient her love feelings non-contingently. Being faithful was not a problem for Cheryl.

Cheryl worked through the issues of commitment and got to the point where she could focus on the practical aspects of fulfillment. Her emotional starting point was a difficult one. Cheryl felt an edge of frustration, loneliness, hurt and anger almost constantly as a wife. While it may seem farfetched to begin working on fulfillment issues when these powerful negative feelings are present, it was just what Cheryl needed to do to get out of her heartbreaking marital slump. Cheryl needed to work on her wife sphere—her color—in the marriage. That's what she was in charge of, not her marriage and not Ed's behavior.

If you are feeling heartbreak in your marriage, you can begin your process for digging out of misery and frustration by following along with Cheryl's progress. Do each step as Cheryl works them out, and a guidance system of action values for your practical fulfillment as a wife will emerge. I will **highlight** the categories you need to think about in order to create your list of action-values as a wife.

CHERYL IDENTIFIES HER ACTION VALUES

In order to start the process of working on fulfillment, I asked Cheryl a question designed to identify her philosophy—her action values—for being a wife. I asked Cheryl, "**What do you want to be like as a married woman no matter to whom you might be married?** Notice,

Cheryl, I am not asking what Ed wants you to be like as a wife, nor what kind of marriage relationship you want to have. The question is about you. Tell me, what comes to mind in terms of how you want to be as a married woman?" The purpose of this question was to begin helping Cheryl identify her philosophy for herself in her marriage. I tape recorded all our sessions so I can report verbatim what we talked about.

I remember that Cheryl thought for a minute and replied, "I want to be loving, caring and faithful." She paused and said, "I want to be respected and loved back."

I interrupted, "Cheryl you said you want to be loving, caring and faithful—that's about you. But when you said you want respect and to be loved, you switched over to what you want your husband to be like. That's a different question. Let's stick with you and what you want to be like as a married woman no matter to whom you might be married. Your values for yourself. Okay?"

"Okay, I think I get it now. That's a hard question. I've never really thought about it."

"I know, most people have not thought much about it. We are conditioned to think more about what we want the other person to be like as though the perfect other will solve all our relationship struggles. The best place to start is with yourself. Does anything more come to mind about what you want to be like as a married woman in the area of connecting?"

"Not really, I think loving, and caring, and faithful, pretty much says it all."

"It certainly says a lot, but let me run some categories by you and see if more doesn't come to mind. How about the category of **attitudes**? What kind of attitudes do you want to carry with you as a wife no matter to whom you are married? Let me give you an example. A wife once told me that when she got home from work, got out of her car and walked down the pathway to her kitchen door, she often asked herself what kind of attitudes she wanted to carry into the house with her. This question helped her shed many of the attitudes that had infiltrated her during the day and to choose attitudes she wanted to have. So, as she walked into her house she tried to connect with her husband and daughter, be attentive, give them both a kiss and ask them how their day went. What comes to your mind about attitudes?"

Cheryl hardly hesitated, and said, "I want to be positive, and...lighthearted, upbeat....sensitive, attentive and trusting. And accepting. I want to be accepting. Yes, that's what I want to be."

I wrote down Cheryl's attitudes on a pad and asked, "How about **communication** as a category? There are two parts to communication, the **sending** part and the **receiving** part. What do you want to be like as a sender of communication as a married woman?"

"I want to express my feelings and thoughts, be assertive—I ran across an old assertiveness book from the 70's recently. It was great. I want to stand up for myself as a wife and be assertive. I want to be open."

"How about as a receiver of communication?"

"I want to be a good listener, and let's see, non-judgmental—I don't like it when others are judgmental of me so I don't want to be that way to them. And, I'd like to be open-minded and understanding."

Next, I asked about her **physical relationship** as a wife. "Cheryl, what do you want to be like in terms of a physical relationship as a married woman?"

"I'm a very physical and intimate person. So, I'd be affectionate, sexual, a good lover, and let's see, intimate, and sexy."

"Would you maybe even like to be romantic?" I asked, good naturedly. "It sounds like you want it all." We both laughed.

"Sure, I want it all. Yeah, I would want to be romantic."

"How about **ethics and morality**, Cheryl. What comes to mind there?"

"Well, I've already said I want to be faithful. That has to do with morality. Let's see, I'd also want to be honest—true to what I say—and trustworthy. It really bugs me when other people lie. I don't want to be like that. That's all I can think of."

"Hey, you're doing great. It's obvious once you hear a category it triggers some really good insights. How about **sharing**? Some wives like to have a lot of individual activities and separate friends, while others like a lot of sharing with a smaller amount of individual stuff. What kind of balance would you like as a wife?"

"I'd like a good balance of individual friends and activities—we don't have to do everything together. I'd never have a friend who wanted to be exclusive with me totally apart from the marriage. That would be uncomfortable. And I don't want to share everything together. It's better if we both have our own things and our shared things. So, I'd want a balance of individual and shared 'stuff,' as you put it." She grins as she mimics my vernacular.

"Here's an interesting category, Cheryl. A bit old fashioned but an important one, nonetheless. What would you want to be like in terms of **manners?**"

Cheryl thinks, "That's important to me. I want to be polite, and let's see, thoughtful, and respectful. I don't like gossip. I think it is often disrespectful. So, yes, I'd be respectful, too."

"Cheryl, how about your **emotions?** How would you want to handle them? What comes to mind?"

Without hesitation, Cheryl say, "I want to be even-tempered. I don't like it when I lose my temper. That's not the way I want to be."

Cheryl's got some momentum, now. She is really into thinking about herself as a married woman and what her values are for herself. I go on with the remaining categories: **household sharing, alcohol or drug use, health and fitness,** and **spirituality.** Cheryl includes on her list, respectively, "share in the household tasks," "be a light social drinker and drug free," "healthy, active, nice looking," and "a good person."

I then ask Cheryl if there is anything we haven't thought of that she wanted to put on her list of values as a wife: A **miscellaneous** category. She said, "Yes, I want to be a friend and companion. These are really important qualities to me as a wife."

This completed Cheryl's list of her action values for being the married woman she wanted to be—her philosophy as a married woman. With her list, Cheryl could begin work on a better marriage with Ed and greater fulfillment as a married woman. She could work on getting back to "her color." By doing this, Cheryl will contribute her true self to the marital mix. This is all she can do; it is her area of power in the marriage.

IDENTIFYING YOUR ACTION VALUES

If you followed along with Cheryl, you may now have a list of your own. If you don't, this is a good place to stop and create your own list of action values. I can't stress enough how important this is. Without a well thought out list of your action values you will not be able to guide yourself through all the emotional twists and turns of everyday marriage. With your list you will be able to begin digging yourself out of hurt, despair and anger. So, go over each of the categories Cheryl used and write down the values that you want to put into your marital life. Don't worry about duplicating ones that are on Cheryl's list. An action value becomes yours when you put it on your list. Nobody can make you put an action value on your list. To help you think of and select action values for you, I am listing a number of action values wives have shared with me over the years. It's an impressive and interesting list. Look it over and if any

BECOMING AN ACTION VALUED MARRIED WOMAN

action value fits you, put it on your list.

Because you will be working from your list to get yourself on track as the wife you want to be, try to keep the size of your list manageable. Cheryl's list includes 38 action values. That's a lot and later Cheryl will eventually trim it down to 13, but for now don't worry too much about how many action values match your philosophy for being a married woman. Put down what you think for now.

MASTER LIST OF ACTION VALUES

Loving	Caring	Supportive
Friend	Companion	Partner
Affectionate	Sexual	Intimate
A good lover	Intriguing	Open
Honest	Faithful	Loyal
Trusting	Trustworthy	Compromise
Truthful	Assertive	Fun
Sense of Humor	Flexible	A lady
Dependable	Reliable	True to self
Considerate	Nice	Active
Out going	Social	Proficient
Interesting	Accepting	Pleasant
Playful	Joyful	Positive
Up-beat	Sensitive	Kind
Forgiving	Intelligent	Thoughtful
Curious	Sociable	Gracious
Courteous	Pretty	Neat
Organized	Polite	Respectful
Welcoming	Attentive	In harmony
Share	Warm	Romantic
Sensible	Open minded	Good listener

Stable	Even	Upright
Even tempered	Good natured	Good homemaker
Patient	Stimulating	Empathetic
Light-hearted	Snugly	Cuddly
Connect	Healthy	Fit
Exercise	Informed	Spiritual
Understanding	A good Christian	Light drinker
Non-drinker	Moderate drinker	Non-smoker
Drug free	True to God	Creative
Up front	Stand up for self	Available

Hostest with the mostest
Strong of Character
Express feelings and thoughts
Share in household tasks
Balance of Individual and Shared Activities

This is not the final list of action values for all time, that is for sure. If you can think of ones not listed, put them down and consider making them yours. Thirty or forty action values are probably about as many as one can effectively keep track of. Don't worry about similarities for now. That will all be sorted out as you see how Cheryl refines her list. As you make your own list of action values, define and clarify each one in your mind. For example, you may have identified "light-hearted" as one of your values. What does this bring to mind? In what ways are you already demonstrating your light-heartedness? What have you learned about yourself that helps you be light hearted? If you put it on your list it means that with a little reflection you will have a clear idea of what it means to you.

BECOMING AN ACTION VALUED MARRIED WOMAN

CHERYL RATES HERSELF

Now that Cheryl had her list, it was time to see how well she was doing as the married woman she wanted to be. It was time for Cheryl to rate herself.

I asked, "Cheryl how would it be if we rated your action values to see how well you have been doing? This will give us a sense of your starting place and help us identify where you are doing well and where you are having a struggle. We can use this scale to do the ratings." I handed Cheryl a note pad with the following scale at the top:

$$-3 \quad -2 \quad -1 \quad 0 \quad +1 \quad +2 \quad +3$$

"This is pretty intimidating," Cheryl responded. "I don't think I will do very well."

"It's just a starting place. What I'll do is read your action values one at a time, and as I do you can write the item down and then rate it using the scale at the top of the note pad. How would it be if we look at the last month as the time frame for doing the rating? Okay?"

"Yeah, sure, why not," Cheryl agreed.

"Let me give you an example of the question to ask yourself as you rate each item. It is kind of an awkward question, but it will help you focus on each action value as you go along. Let's look at your first action value, 'loving.' The question you want to ask yourself is: 'how well have I been loving in the last month, compared to the way I want to be loving, as the married woman I want to be?' So, as you write down the action value of 'loving,' what rating would you give it?"

Cheryl asked me, "What do you mean by 'loving?'"

"It can have a hundred meanings, Cheryl, but the one that counts is yours. It means what it means to you. When you think of yourself as being loving the way you want to be loving, that's what 'loving' means to you. That's the 'loving' you will be rating."

Cheryl stopped to reflect and to look at the rating scale. "Okay, I understand. So, I am to rate myself on how well I have been doing compared to the way I want to be as a wife, is that right?"

I nodded my head. Cheryl wrote down 'loving' and said, "I'll rate that a -2, I haven't been very loving in the last month compared with the way I would want to be. More like a frustrated bitch, if the truth be known."

"How about 'caring.' How would you rate it?"

"Well, about the same. Oh dear, this is going to look awful. I've not done a very good job, have I?"

"Let's wait and see. Most people find that on some action values they are pretty far off track, while on others they are doing well. For instance, how about 'faithful,' the next action value on your list. How would you rate it?"

"Oh, that's better. That's a +3. Through it all, I've not felt like looking for someone else."

Next, I asked Cheryl about being positive over the last month. She rated herself a 0 on being positive. She said the 0 meant that she was neither positive nor negative but somewhere in between, so she rated it a 0. I asked her if she could give an example of when she was "somewhat positive" in the past month? She said she had not given up on the whole thing, and that seemed somewhat positive, but that she wasn't walking around with a positive attitude, either.

"How about 'light-hearted?' I asked. Cheryl rated that a 0, as well. Again, I asked if there was even a bit of evidence that she was light hearted, and she answered, "I haven't lost my ability to laugh—at least in here."

"The next one on your list is 'upbeat.' How would you rate it?"

"Oh, that's a -1. I have been a sort of sourpuss over the last month. I think it is my hurt. It's hard feeling hurt all the time and not showing it."

Cheryl rated "sensitive" a +1 and then I asked her about "attentive."

"Oh, I'll give that a -3. I've been really withdrawn from Ed for months now. I hardly pay any attention to him. Just the opposite, I ignore him for the most part. I'm about as off track with 'attentive' as I can get."

Cheryl went on to rate her remaining action values. This is how all of her ratings turned out:

CHERYL'S RATINGS OF HER ACTION VALUES

Loving	-2	Caring	-2
Faithful	+3	Positive	0
Light-hearted	0	Upbeat	-1
Sensitive	+1	Attentive	-3
Trusting	+1	Accepting	-2
Assertive	0	Express feelings and thougthts	-2
Open	-1	Good listener	-2
Honest	+2	Open minded	-1
Understanding	-2	Affectionate	-2
Sexual	-3	A good lover	-3
Intimate	-3	Sexy	-1
Romantic	-3	Non-judgmental	-2
Trustworthy	+3	Balance of individual and shared activities	-2
Polite	0	Even tempered	-1
Respectful	-1	Share in household tasks	+2
Drug free	+3	Light social drinker	+3
Healthy	+1	Active	+1

THE MARRIED WOMAN

| Nice looking | +1 | A good person | +2 |
| Friend | -2 | Companion | -2 |

Based on Cheryl's own ratings of her action values as a married woman, it is not surprising she feels miserable in her marriage to Ed. Cheryl is seriously off track with herself as the married woman she wants to be—her wife sphere has become a color that is not working for her. She is not managing her wife sphere well, the only place in the marriage where she has power. There is no way she can feel good about being a married woman as off track as she is with the color of being the wife she wants to be.

The majority of Cheryl's action values are negative. She is *off track* with her own action values for being loving, caring, upbeat, attentive, accepting, expressing her feelings and thoughts, open, a good listener, non-judgmental, open minded, understanding, affectionate, sexual, a good lover, intimate, sexy, romantic, maintaining a balance of individual and shared activities, respectful, even-tempered, and a friend and a companion, as a wife. Despite the distress she feels in the marriage, Cheryl is <u>neutral</u>—neither on track nor off track— on four action values: positive, light-hearted, assertive and polite. And bravely, she is <u>on track</u> on several important action values: Cheryl is faithful, sensitive, trusting, honest, trustworthy, sharing in household activities, drug free, a light social drinker, healthy, active, nice looking, and a good person, as a wife.

If Cheryl wants to feel good about herself as a married woman and put positive energy into the marriage, she must find a way to get herself on track—to color her wife sphere according to her action values. She must be honest and accepting about her difficult starting place and develop a strategy to get herself to where she wants to be. Her present ratings give her a clear idea of her difficult starting point. Her specific

BECOMING AN ACTION VALUED MARRIED WOMAN

definitions of her values will help guide her to the behaviors and attitudes she is now missing. Those same definitions will help her picture what she'll be doing differently when she is on track. Her list, on the whole, allows her to know what to focus on to get herself there. As you will see, Cheryl's commitment to her action values becomes the heart and soul of who she is as a married woman. She will learn how to guide herself from her list. She will find her unique color for being the wife she wants to be. But it will be an incredibly difficult struggle at times.

I asked Cheryl what she thought of her ratings.

"I feel pretty horrible. I had no idea I was so far off track with myself. I don't know if I can do this. It seems like a huge job to get on track."

"I agree, if you look at your whole list, it is a huge job. I have some ideas though. First, is there someplace where you can put the list so that you see it often? I think it will help if you increase your awareness of specifically how you want to be a married woman, your philosophy for yourself—that's what the list is. If you put the list someplace where you will see it often, this will help you increase your awareness. I have found that becoming aware of your action values is the groundwork for starting to work on them. Second, it will help if you choose two or three action values on which to get started. Choose ones on which you rated yourself negatively—as being off track—and ones that you think if you were to experience progress, you would feel better about yourself in your marriage."

Cheryl said, "I could type up the list and put it on the inside of the visor of my car. I drive someplace everyday. That way, when I wait at stop signs or in traffic, I can flip the visor down and glance over the list. As far as choosing two or three action values to get started on, I don't know." Cheryl paused and looked at her list. "It would be too hard to start with intimacy. My feelings are too hurt and I don't want to deal with that kind of rejection right now. How about if I choose one in the middle, like 'positive,' and two more in which I'm off track, like 'accepting' and 'attentive'? Boy, would Ed be surprised if I came home being positive, accepting and attentive." Cheryl managed a nervous laugh at this idea.

"Well, I like your idea of putting your list on the visor of your car. Very creative. I can see you driving around looking for stop lights so you can stop and look up at your list." We both chuckled at this image. "And becoming more positive, accepting and attentive, I think is a great way to start getting on track as the wife you want to be."

CHERYL BEGINS TO GET ON TRACK

Cheryl agreed to try to focus on her selected action values for one week, independent of what Ed was like as a husband, and then come back and tell me what she learned. She would focus on herself and getting on track with her selected action values, and not on Ed or what he was doing, or not doing, as a husband. A tough assignment, but Cheryl was willing to give it a try.

Cheryl came back the next week very discouraged. She felt she had not done well at all. I asked her to rate her three action values. She rated them, positive: 0, accepting: -1, and attentive: -1. While Cheryl had improved from -2's to -1's, she remained off track. I asked her what had happened.

"I went home all pepped up and ready to try. I started by being attentive. Before dinner, I asked Ed if I could get him anything, a drink or something. He was particularly sullen. He said, 'no' as though I didn't exist. I went ahead and fixed a little snack and offered that to him. He just looked at it, nibbled a little bit, didn't say anything, and got up, walked into the family room and turned on the TV. I got mad. But, I kept quiet. I thought to myself, I would remain positive no matter what. I fixed dinner, put it on the table and told Ed that it was ready. Ed yelled back from the family room that he wasn't hungry. That's when I lost it. I went into the family room and told him what a jerk he was and that from now on he could fix his own damn dinner. He yelled back that he didn't have to eat if he didn't want to. He told me to get off his case. I went back to the dining room table and started eating with the kids. Pretty soon, Ed came in and said he was sorry. He sat down and we finished our dinner. I ignored him. I was too hurt to talk. I turned all my attention to the kids. They were being overly quiet. They're really good kids. I put a lot of effort into being pleasant with them, I guess partly to show Ed what he's missing and because I don't want them to suffer because of our fighting. The kids and I talked while Ed ate in silence. When dinner was over Ed went back to his TV and I cleaned up. The rest of the night was business as usual—I spent time with the kids and Ed watched TV. The rest of the week went pretty much the same. I'm feeling pretty discouraged and hopeless. I tried, I really did and it didn't seem to do any good."

Cheryl's feelings are not unusual. She felt discouraged about being off track—and she had been—some of the week. But I suspect she was also discouraged because her efforts had not caught Ed's attention and changed his behavior. Digging yourself out of the destructive patterns of a troubled marriage is difficult. Being positive, accepting and attentive when you don't feel like it, is hard emotional work. In order to address her action values and her feelings, Cheryl needed to learn that feelings and actions can be separated. This can give her greater control over her actions and make her better able to connect them to her values without discounting her feelings.

I asked Cheryl how she would know if she were, for instance, accepting when Ed is withdrawn and rude?

She thought about this. "I guess I would just let him be. I know he is not feeling good about himself. He really is one-dimensional about his business. He measures himself as a person only by the way his business goes. I understand it, but I don't like it. I guess I would just ignore his mood and do what I think is right. You know, stop reacting to him."

"So, you would understand what motivates his moods and you would let him be. What else would you do if you were accepting in the way you want to be accepting, if you were getting on track?"

"I guess I would listen. Let him get things off his chest. Let him vent if he wants. And, I would let him be alone if he wants to be. I'd respect his need for time to himself. I wouldn't follow him around and try to get him to talk. I'd still do nice things for him. I would ask him if he would like some coffee when I fix myself some. Things like that."

I enjoyed Cheryl's insights. "So you know what to do to be accepting and attentive when Ed withdraws and gets moody. But, what do you feel like doing when Ed withdraws or is rude?"

"Well, I have mixed feelings. I feel like crying, I feel like criticizing, I feel like screaming, I feel like giving up. I feel all these things."

"What do you do when you have these feelings?"

"I used to try to get him to talk. I'd get so frustrated I would end up yelling a lot. I was incredibly angry with his withdrawn and negative moods. I don't yell so much anymore. Now, I'm more likely to withdraw myself. I try to ignore him. It seems to hurt less that way," Cheryl replied.

"It's normal to have the feelings you describe when Ed withdraws into himself and becomes emotionally unavailable. You get frustrated, angry and hurt. That is perfectly natural, no question about it, but—here's the question—is it working for you? To let these feelings dictate what you are like as a wife won't work. It is best if you guide yourself from your action values, your list, rather than from these temporary feelings. You need to learn to separate your feelings from your actions so you can guide your actions from your values and not from feelings that won't work."

Cheryl got a look of dismay on her face. "You mean I should just stuff my feelings and be accepting?" she said.

"Well, yes and no," I said. "Yes, I think you should be accepting even though you don't feel like it, and no, I don't think you should stuff your feelings. Let me put it this way. As parents we tell our children that it is all right to feel angry—anger is a normal feeling—but it is not okay to hit, scream, bite, throw things or fall on the floor and flail your legs about in the air when you are angry. We are telling our kids that it is okay to feel anger but it not okay to direct their anger into inappropriate behaviors. We are telling them to separate their feelings from their actions. We expect them to learn to experience feelings and to know they feel them but to manage their feelings while directing their behavior according to higher values. In essence we are teaching them to stay on track even though they may not feel like it."

Cheryl said, "I never thought of it that way. So, it is okay for me to feel angry and hurt—that's normal—but when I do I should stay on track and be accepting anyway, even though I don't feel like it?"

"Yes, that is exactly what I mean. You are fun to work with. You catch on so quickly. In some circles, this "technique" of directing your behavior according to your values while managing your feelings so they don't head you in the wrong direction, is called emotional intelligence. To just give in to your feelings as an adult woman doesn't work. It can't 'get you there' as a wife. It especially won't work as you try to dig yourself out of a miserable marital spot. If you keep doing what you've always done, you'll keep getting what you've always gotten. If you want to get something different in your marital life, you must do something different." I said.

Cheryl nodded, "It sounds hard. I don't know if I can do it."

"Nobody does it all the time, at least nobody I know. Everybody gets off track. If you can do it even part of the time, you will make a nice discovery. You will find out that when you are accepting, even though you don't feel like it, some of the feelings of anger and hurt will dissipate. You will begin to shed these feelings. This will allow other feelings to take their place, feelings that are a lot easier to handle. Feelings like compassion and empathy. You will be like a boat that stays its course. If you look back you will see that the boat makes a wake but that the wake smoothes out on its own as it trails behind the boat. Contrast this with a boat that turns and turns, bouncing up and down in its own wake. Now, that is a boat in trouble. As long as it continuously turns, it will create its own wake and be thrown about by it. That's what it is like when you have angry, hurt feelings and let them dictate what you are like as a wife. Acting out your feelings turns you in a circle, bouncing you up and down in the emotions of the moment. As a wife, you have the same emotional experience over and over. It's no fun. Know what I mean?" I asked. .

Cheryl shook her head in agreement. "I've made a lot of those turnarounds, and I've been bouncing up and down in those waves for a long time. I know how bad that feels. Like a circle of discontent that you never get out of. You feel bad all the time."

Cheryl now understands that in order to get on track she will have to behave in ways she doesn't feel. She now understands that she can acknowledge her feelings but separately guide herself from her action values. She is acquiring wisdom about how feelings and actions interact and about the process she can follow for digging herself out of the present anguish she feels as a wife. While Cheryl learns to stay on track by being positive, attentive, and accepting, even though she may not feel like it, she is laying the groundwork for important work on the other action values she listed. Learning that she is not controlled by temporary feelings of hurt and anger can release Cheryl to work on higher order reasons to be who she wants to be, namely from her values. This will help Cheryl take charge and create the color she chooses for being a wife.

Cheryl came back the next week looking quite pleased with herself. For the first time, I could see some pride radiating from a pleased grin on her face. I asked her how she had done getting herself on track with the three action values she targeted, especially being accepting. She described how she went home and really readied herself for Ed's sullenness and withdrawal. She said to me, "Poor Ed, he didn't know what to do. No matter what he did, I was nice. If he sat in silence and watched TV, I sat there with him. When I got up to get something, I asked if he wanted something. Whether he said yes or no, I was pleasant. I asked him how his business was going. He told me how things were still bad but maybe getting a little better. I listened. I didn't fidget or busy myself with some household thing, I just paid attention to what he was saying. When he went to his bedroom and I went to mine, I kissed his cheek and said 'good night.' Although I felt disappointed that Ed didn't seem to notice my attentiveness, I remembered what you said about my being in charge of what I do, even when I don't feel like doing it. This helped and I think I stayed on track pretty well."

"Cheryl, what did you find out about separating feelings from actions, about keeping your boat on course?"

"I think I know what you mean now," Cheryl said. "If I follow my anger and hurt feelings I will just stay stuck. I'll just continue to be the hurt and wretched wife I've been over and over again. But if I can get on track as the wife I want to be, I can actually feel better. When I was pleasant to Ed, I felt better. I didn't feel like what he was doing was controlling my behavior. I felt more in charge of myself and my emotions. I must say part of me enjoyed surprising Ed. I just didn't react to his withdrawal. In fact, I began to feel sorry for him. The poor guy really is miserable."

"Wow, Cheryl, good job! I'll bet Ed is a little surprised. Let's see how you rate on the action values you targeted."

Cheryl's rating reflected her progress. She scored ratings of a +2 on positive, +2 on attentive and +2 accepting! This was quite an improvement from the -2 scores she had given herself on these action values one month ago. Cheryl was beginning to take charge of her color as a wife.

"So, you were able to do it, to be more like you want to be, while not reacting to Ed and getting off track with yourself. How did this feel to you as a wife?"

I asked Cheryl this question to help her focus on the new overall experience she has of herself as a wife. In order to feel more pride and confidence as a married woman, Cheryl must develop a sense of what she is doing well and not so well. This allows for self-correction. She must reflect on herself and know she is in charge of herself as a wife. Ed can make it hard, or easy, for her to be the wife she wants to be, but he will never be in charge of her, she is. The more aware Cheryl is that she is in charge and the more aware she is of her specific action values, the better she will be at staying on track, especially when negative feelings and the desire to react to Ed, make it hard.

"I felt good about myself. I felt like I was learning something new and valuable, and finding out that it can work for me. I don't think I am where I want to be, but I found out I can do it. I feel more hopeful," Cheryl said.

"Well, you got a good start. You've gone from being off track, to being on track, on these action values. Keep in mind that you won't always be able to stay on track in every situation and marital moment. No wife—or husband—is on track all the time. Just do your best for now and get as good as you can at getting on track," I said.

Obviously, Cheryl was feeling more pride in herself as a married woman than she has in a long time. She was learning that she can be in charge of herself by managing her actions separately from her momentary feelings. She does not have to react to her feelings nor to Ed's behaviors. Cheryl is developing a pathway she can follow that will help her get out of the miserable reaction patterns she has been in. By getting on track with her action values, this new course will allow her to move in the direction of pride and fulfillment as a wife. But, like Cheryl said, she is not there yet, as we shall see.

Next, I asked Cheryl to choose two or three additional action values to focus on for the next week. She looked over her list: "I think I'll choose 'light-hearted'—I'm tired of being morose; it doesn't fit my character anyway. And, I'll work on being affectionate and being a friend. I've been very distant from Ed for months now. It's no fun."

"Those are good choices. They will certainly challenge your feelings. You'll get some more practice separating your feelings from your actions. It looks as though you like challenges once you get going. Do you think, in your marriage at present, you are feeling more hurt and anger or more hopeful and positive?"

"It's still hard. I still feel hurt and angry. I don't expect to get over these feelings right away. Maybe I shouldn't choose these action values. Maybe I should slow down," Cheryl said.

"Well that's a thought. I just want you to keep in mind that your starting place is a difficult one no matter which action values you choose to work on. Anger and hurt are lurking in your emotional bank account, and I know you won't feel like being light-hearted, a friend, and affectionate. You've been feeling miserable for a long time now. How will you do it, you know, get started with these action values, if you decide to go ahead with them?"

"I'll try to do what I did with being pleasant and accepting. I'm going to be light-hearted, a friend, and affectionate even though I don't feel like it. I'll just make myself do it. Maybe better feelings will just come along on their own," Cheryl said with determination and a growing confidence. "And, I'll just steel myself from reacting to Ed when he is so distant and irritable. After all, I'm in charge of what I'm like as a wife, Ed isn't," she said with a knowing look.

Again, I enjoyed Cheryl's insights. She was beginning to understand how she got off track by reacting to Ed's negative moods. What has happened to Cheryl in her marriage to Ed occurs in many marriages that have gone awry. In Cheryl's marriage, Ed reacts to his business worries by becoming irritable and withdrawn. Cheryl reacts to Ed's moods by feeling hurt and angry. The more Ed withdraws, the more Cheryl gets angry and critical. The more Cheryl gets angry and critical, the more Ed withdraws or bursts out of his isolation with angry words of his own. Pretty soon, Cheryl feels hurt, angry and emotionally abandoned. She no longer feels like being attentive, positive, affectionate, and loving. She stops trying. She gets stuck. She feels hopeless. If she follows her hurt and hopeless feelings, she will remain withdrawn and uninvolved. She doesn't feel like being close, so she isn't. She becomes an active participant in the withdrawal and isolation characterizing her marriage. She even initiates her own move into a separate bedroom.

Cheryl is learning a way to get unstuck. She is finding out that she can get on track and not react to Ed's moods, and that she can be on track even though she doesn't feel like it. She is learning that initiating actions can change feelings, and that she is in charge of how she acts, not Ed. He can only make it hard or easy for her to be on track or not. I think Cheryl intuitively knew all this but she hadn't been doing it.

"What are you going to do, Cheryl, if you express affection but Ed rejects you? What if you attempt to hold his hand or kiss him and he turns away?" I asked.

Cheryl got a knowing look in her eyes and replied, "I know that will happen. I'm ready for it. When it does, I'll get some practice being positive and accepting, won't I? After all, I can express affection independently of Ed. It won't be much fun if he doesn't respond at all, but I think he will eventually. I'll just stick with my actions as long as I can."

Cheryl is right. While she is not in charge of whether affection is reciprocated, she is in charge of whether she expresses affection on her own initiative. Too often, spouses forget that they are in charge of the action part of interaction. They think, "when he doesn't reciprocate, I have to stop initiating," and "when he doesn't accept my affection, I have to stop being affectionate." This belief results in a withdrawal and shutting down of valuable contributions to the relationship, such as individually directed affection. Cheryl is catching on what it means to be independent and in charge of her participation in her marriage. She can express affection independently of Ed's response. It won't be easy, but it can be done. In order for her to get back to her color as the wife she wants to be, she will have to initiate her own actions as a wife, independently of Ed.

I wanted to further help Cheryl get concrete ideas in her mind for work on being on track with her newly targeted action values. "How will you know if you are affectionate? What will you be doing that indicates to you that you are being affectionate?"

"Well, I think that's pretty obvious. I'll touch him more, and I'll kiss him on the cheek, maybe even on the lips."

"What do you mean, you will touch him more?" I asked.

"Things like, putting my arm through his when we are walking or hold his hand. I'll sit on the arm of his chair for a moment or two when he's watching TV and put my arm around his shoulders. I'll kiss him good night when I go to my room. Things like that," she said.

"You also said you want to become more lighthearted and friendly. How will you know when you are being like this?"

"I think that will be harder than being affectionate. I can just make myself be affectionate, but being light hearted and friendly, they seem a little more abstract to me. Let's see." I could see Cheryl's mind working and images forming. "To be lighthearted, I'm just going to have do an attitude adjustment. I've been carrying so much anger and hurt around, that I've become a sourpuss on my own. I think I'll try to ignore my anger—set it to one side for awhile—and get back to being bouncy. I've always had a lot of good energy, a kind of peppy person. Then the marriage got bad and I got downhearted along with it. I'm just going to lighten up, quit complaining and stop walking around looking like one of Ed's trucks ran over my heart. I'll probably smile more."

"Sounds good to me," I said. "But how about being more of a friend? How are you going to do that?"

"That I know how to do, I've just not been doing it. I know that Ed is worried sick about his business. It has really affected him. If I had a big worry in my life and one of my friends knew about it, she would try to understand and sympathize with me. My friend would give me support and help me to believe in myself. That's what I need to do with Ed. I need to understand how worried he is and support him. He must feel pretty abandoned by me just the way I feel abandoned by him. I'm going to help Ed believe in himself, that he is okay even if his business isn't," Cheryl said.

"So, if I understand it, Cheryl, you are going to get yourself on track by being affectionate, lighthearted and a friend, in the way you are a wife in your marriage. Plus, you are going to continue to be on track being positive, attentive, and accepting. Is that right?" I asked.

Cheryl got a mischievous look on her face, and said, "Yea, Ed won't know what hit him, will he?"

Cheryl agreed to continue working on being positive, accepting and attentive, and to add lighthearted, affectionate and "being a friend" to her efforts to get on track. We agreed to meet in two weeks to find out what she had been able to accomplish.

Cheryl was getting a bit cocky. That's okay. I knew from experience that she would suffer a setback and when that happened it would be my job to make it a positive part of all that she was learning about how to be married successfully. I was hoping the setback wouldn't occur for a few more session so that Cheryl could continue to build her confidence. Confidence is like emotional money in the bank, and during a setback Cheryl would be able to draw on it. The more in her savings account, the more she could draw on.

MARRIAGE MAKEOVER

STEP NINE

Getting on Track Sexually

*I want to be sexual but
I don't feel like it.*

When I next saw Cheryl I asked her how it went. She was still feeling confident and proud. She told me, "I think I did a good job. And, I moved back into the bedroom with Ed."

I asked her why she started sleeping with her husband again. "Well, you know, I began to understand that I'm off track as the wife I want to be if I'm not sleeping with my husband, so I decided to get myself on track and start sleeping with him."

"Cheryl, what was Ed's response to your returning to bed with him?"

"He didn't say anything. He wasn't negative about it—he didn't push me away or tell me to go back to my room—but he wasn't openly accepting, either. I mean, he didn't want to snuggle in bed or lie together and talk. At this stage, I'm not expecting much, so I'll see where it goes," Cheryl said.

What Cheryl did is not uncommon. As a wife begins to understand that she is responsible for choosing to be married, she begins to get clearer and more focused on herself, who she wants to be as a wife, what will work for her, and she begins doing it. Not only is Cheryl's list of action values helping guide her as a wife, but so is her awareness about who she wants to be as a wife. It is as if Cheryl were separating her marital experience into two marriages, the one that didn't work—the one in which she was off track, miserable, withdrawn, angry and hurt—and the one that is taking shape in which she is on track through the strong presence of her own values. In order to move into this restructured marriage, she must separate herself from the feelings created by the marriage that didn't work so that she doesn't just recreate that marriage over and over as she experiences the negative feelings of that marriage and acts them out. Also, she must continue to act in ways that are consistent with her values for being a wife so her new way of being married can take root. The old marriage, the one that didn't work, was based on the feelings it created, while her new way of being married is based on Cheryl's action values and the positive feelings emerging from being on track. Cheryl was finding her color again. It was nice to see.

"What was Ed's reaction to your sleeping with him?" I asked. "Weren't you taking a chance that he would reject you and ask you to move back to your room?"

"I thought of that," Cheryl said, "but I thought it was worth the risk. Besides, I wanted this to be about me. I didn't want to think, 'I will get rejected,' and then stay stuck. I wanted to get on track with who I want to be. So, I did it," Cheryl said with a show of satisfaction in her voice.

"Well, did either of you get smoochy in bed, or did you just sleep together?" I asked.

"We just slept together. I kissed him good night. One night I even gave him a short kiss on the lips. I think that really surprised him. It was fun surprising him like that. He didn't turn away. He seemed okay about it. In fact, after about five nights, he told me it was nice having me back. That's the first encouraging thing I've heard from him in weeks. It was nice to hear."

"Well, nice job, Cheryl. I like that you extended yourself on your own. And, I'm glad it turned out so well. Even though you are in charge of you, it is nice to hear something encouraging from your husband, isn't it?"

It's hard for Ed not to respond when Cheryl stops reacting to him and becomes positive on her own. While I will try to keep Cheryl focused on herself and not Ed's reactions, I know that as Cheryl gets more and more on track it will be easier for Ed to come out of his shell. Ed has been, and pretty much continues to be quite miserable. But he's not made of stone. It is nice for Cheryl to see that not only is she feeling better because she is getting on track, but that Ed is noticing her changes. Cheryl is contributing positively to the "marital inbetween" and Ed is experiencing her pleasantness and he is responding to it. His positive reaction then goes into their marital inbetween and Cheryl experiences that. This is the way a better marriage occurs—a better marital inbetween emerges. If both Ed and Cheryl were in therapy together, we could work on mutual contributions to their inbetween. Since Ed refuses to come in, Cheryl must do what she can do to feel better. And, she is doing it quite well, so far.

"Cheryl, how did you do on the three action values you chose to emphasize over the last two weeks? I think they were lighthearted, affectionate and being a friend."

"I think I did better. I put them on the visor in my car and looked at them a lot. Whenever I got out of the car to go into the house, I was pretty primed."

"Did Ed ever make it really hard for you? Did he give you a challenge?"

"Well, sort of. Generally, he was not too reactive. He let me put my arm through his when we walked, but he never encouraged it. One time we were sitting on the couch watching TV and I put my arm around his shoulders and he moved slightly away, enough to let me know he didn't want me to do that. But other times he was okay about it," Cheryl replied.

"What did you do when he didn't respond well or moved away? I bet you didn't feel like being close to him then. It must have hurt to have him pull away and be so unresponsive most of the time. Did you feel like pulling away yourself?"

"I didn't feel like being close. I was hurt and I did feel like withdrawing. I even found myself beginning to react. When he pulled away from me for putting my arm around his shoulder, my instant reaction was to get upset and move to a chair and stop sitting by him, just to show him I didn't like what he did. But I've learned that I just can't let these reactive feelings overwhelm me as a wife. All that does is get me stuck in the very feelings I don't want to experience any longer. Besides, focusing on being a friend again has helped me. I thought of what a friend would do. I just took my arm back and continued to sit next to him. When the TV show ended, I asked him about work and the business, and I listened. I began encouraging him. I told him that I believed in him; that I've always admired his ability to solve problems, and that I knew he would solve this one too. I think he liked hearing this. It made me feel good to say it. Then we went to bed, I kissed him good night and we went to sleep. Before I fell asleep I thought how much better it felt to let go of my hurt and stay on track than it did to react and withdraw," Cheryl said.

Cheryl's ability to manage her reactive feelings and decide what to do, and perhaps more important, what not to do based on her action values, shows a change in *modus operandi* as a married woman from what I call, "Feel-*Act*-Think," to "Feel-*Think*-Act." Feel-*Act*-Think doesn't work well in a marriage. It means your husband does something that negatively affects you, you react (usually negatively) and then you consider what you did or could have done differently. This mode of being a wife sets up circular battles with him saying something critical, you getting hurt and being critical in return, him getting louder in his counter-criticism, you becoming louder, both of you withdrawing, licking your wounds, waiting for the next go around.

Feel-*Think*-Act means your husband expresses something critical, you feel like reacting negatively, but instead, you consider what you want to be like as a wife independently of your husband's actions and your momentary feelings. You do what you think is best by guiding your behavior from the higher order place of your action values. Cheryl is learning that it is best to be aware of what she feels, what she wants to be like as a wife, and to stay on track rather than reacting just because she feels like it. Cheryl is learning to guide herself from her values rather than from emotional reactions that do not serve her well. Cheryl's Feel-*Think*-Act mode makes her less a victim of her feelings, her moods and her reactions to Ed. It puts her more in charge of herself.

"Does Ed seem as withdrawn and angry as he has in the past?" I asked.

"Not as much," Cheryl replied. "He seems a little more easy going. I can't tell if it's because his business looks better—our money situation seems to be improving— or if he is just being nicer. Whatever the reason, he is more pleasant to be around. He's talking more, he's spending more time with us, and he doesn't seem so morose. The kids are noticing it too. They told me dad is nicer to them. I think he is more connected to us than he has been."

"Has Ed asked you about the work you are doing in seeing me? Has he seemed to notice some of the changes you are making," I asked?

"He hasn't said much but I think he's noticing some of the more obvious things, like my sleeping with him again, and sitting next to him when we watch TV, stuff like that. I told him I planned to continue seeing you and that I was working on me. He didn't say much to that."

Cheryl's answers confirmed my thoughts that their marital inbetween was improving—becoming less negative and more positive. Putting more of her chosen color into the marital inbetween was changing it, and Ed's more positive response was helping. But I knew I needed to continue to stress the importance that Cheryl stay focused on what she is like as a wife. A wife (and a husband) can get into measuring how well she is doing by the yardstick of how happy or upset her husband may be. I didn't want Cheryl to slip into this kind of emotional dependency. I was worried that Cheryl was beginning to float as a wife. She had learned a lot, experienced mostly success at it, and was becoming somewhat complacent about being on track. She was treating the process of getting on track as something fairly easy to do. I knew she was in for a test pretty soon, but I didn't know in what form it would occur.

We rated the action values Cheryl had been focusing on so far in her attempt to get on track. This is how she rated herself: positive +2, accepting +2, attentive +2, lighthearted +1, affectionate +1, and being a friend +1. We further decided to rate all of the remainingaction values on her list. Often times, when some action values improve others do as well. There is a kind of consolidating effect among all the action values.

CHERYL RATES HER ACTION VALUES

Loving	+1		Caring	+1
Faithful	+3		Positive	+2
Light hearted	+1		Up beat	+1
Sensitive	+2		Attentive	+2
Trusting	+2		Accepting	+2
Assertive	+1		Express feelings and thoughts	+1
Open	+1		Good listener	+2
Active	+2		Open minded	+2
Understanding	+2		Affectionate	+1
Sexual	-2		A good lover	-3

Intimate	0	Sexy	-2
Romantic	-2	Honest	+3
Trustworthy	+3	Balance of individual and shared activities	0
Polite	+2	Respectful	+2
Even tempered	+2	Share in household tasks	+2
Drug free	+3	Light social drinker	+3
Healthy	+2	Non-judgmental	+1
Nice looking	+1	A good person	+3
Friend	+1	Companion	+1

When Cheryl first rated her action values, they were mostly negative. Now they are mostly positive. She is clearly getting on track as the wife she wants to be. She is learning how to be a wife in a way that works for her. She is managing her wife space better. It is no surprise that she feels better now because she is operating from the only place in her marriage where she has power. It is also not surprising she feels more positive about herself and more hopeful about her marriage with Ed. So far, things have gone fairly well for her in her work to get on track.

Cheryl and I examined her list. It was obvious she was on track in most areas except sexual intimacy. I asked her what she thought about this.

"Wow, that's a scary area. I haven't felt like having sex for a long time and I'm not sure Ed would want me. Even sleeping together he has shown no interest. I'm not sure how I feel. It's been so long. There is no groove there like there once was. We've spent so much time withdrawing and being angry, there has been no interest in sex. I'm not sure I'm ready

GETTING ON TRACK SEXUALLY

for this," Cheryl said with a slight shudder.

"Cheryl, you say you don't feel like being sexual. Where do you think that feeling comes from? When and where did it get started?" I asked.

I could see Cheryl become reflective. Then she said, "I guess I stopped feeling sexually close to Ed when he started withdrawing from me. Then it got worse when we started fighting and I moved into a separate bedroom. The last thing I wanted then was for him to touch me. I was too angry and hurt. Now I'm starting to feel better about Ed. But I don't know if I'm ready for that kind of closeness."

I could tell by Cheryl's comments how uncertain she felt about sex with Ed because of the way she avoided the specific mention of sex, when she referred to it as, "touching me," and "that kind of closeness." When people feel anxious about a specific area of life they usually use language that keeps them linguistically distanced from the object of anxiety. I know that Cheryl's language will change as she becomes more comfortable with the idea of being sexual with Ed and learns how to get on track in this area of her marriage.

"So, Cheryl, the feeling of not wanting to be sexually involved with Ed comes from the feelings you have had in the marriage that has not worked. If you had a successful marriage, how would you feel about sexual intimacy with Ed?" I asked.

"Well, if we had a successful marriage, we would be closer and intimate, and having sex, and I would feel like it," Cheryl said. "But, I think I know where you're going with this. You're going to say that I must separate my feelings about not wanting sex from my actions of having sex because my negative feelings come from an unsuccessful marriage and will perpetuate it if I continue to follow my feelings and not have sex." Cheryl looked quite proud of herself for figuring this out. I was proud of her, too.

I joked with her, "Cheryl, would you like to change chairs. Maybe you should sit where I am instead of me. I really like it that you can apply the principle of separating feelings from actions. You've seen how you have to do things you may not feel like doing if you are going to pull yourself out of the hurt and dismay of the marriage that isn't working. You're right; if you follow the feelings of the unhappy marriage you will continue that marriage. You will turn, and turn, in a circle of unhappiness. While it makes sense to put actions before feelings when you are trying to get on track, I know how hard it is to apply this insight to sex and make yourself initiate sex if you don't fully feel like it. That is one of the hardest thing I see wives do as they get on track—initiate sex when they don't feel like it. Maybe it would help if you connect being sexual with the logic of making a choice to be married. Connect being sexual to this idea: No one can make you be married but you. You want to feel fulfilled in your marriage. No matter to whom you would be married you would be sexual—it's a value of yours—so in this marriage if you want it to be successful you will want to be sexual. In other words, if you are going to be married, be sexual. It's part of how you will fulfill yourself as a married woman. Don't have sex and you will not be the wife you want to be, and you will be less fulfilled as a married woman. When you don't feel like being sexual because you have become hurt in your marriage, it is imperative that you become sexual even though you don't feel like it in order to break out of the circle that is not working for you. If you are an adult choosing to be married, then it will only make sense to work on being successfully married. We both know that feelings can follow actions—that by becoming sexual you can nourish the feelings of sexual intimacy. Does this make sense?" I asked.

"I know exactly what you're saying and I agree. I've tried it and I know it works. It's just so hard. What if Ed rejects me? I don't know if I can handle that."

I could see that Cheryl's fears remained. In order to get her grounded

GETTING ON TRACK SEXUALLY

in real images, I asked Cheryl, "How will you know if you are being sexual? What will you do and by doing it know that you are being sexual?"

Cheryl thought for a moment and said, "I would go to bed naked. That used to be a sure sign to Ed that I wanted sexual intimacy with him. I could do that. I would snuggle with him in bed. I would sit close to him after the kids go to bed. I could tell him how much I miss being close to him. I could kiss him on the lips more. I could also tell him I would like to have sex and ask if he is interested. Things like that," she said with a knowing look. She knew if she initiated these actions, sex would probably occur with Ed.

"So, you know what to do in order to initiate sexually intimate actions on your part, and also to ask Ed if he wants sex. I think you are right. All the things you mentioned are good ideas. But, what if Ed rejects you. What will you do then?"

"I'll probably call you late at night and give you the business for getting me into this. (Little did Cheryl know how prophetic this offhand comment turned out to be!) Really, if he rejects me I'll retreat—I know I will—then I'll lick my wounds, probably talk to myself about who I am and what I want to be like and try to get myself back on track. I know what I have to do if I want to break this awful circle I've been in for the last year. Whatever I have to do to get out of that kind of unhappiness is worth the effort. It's awful being married day after day feeling angry and hurt. I'm going to get on track if it kills me," Cheryl said with a determined grin.

Cheryl bolstered her courage by getting clear in her mind how she was going to be affectionate and sexual. That's where change begins, with ideas and images in your mind. Cheryl knows what she needs to do and she is determined to do it. We agreed to get together again in two weeks to review her progress.

MARRIAGE MAKEOVER

STEP TEN

Surviving Set Backs

*How to stick with your action values
when your feelings are hurt.*

BEFORE THE TWO WEEKS WERE UP, one evening at about 9:30, I got a call at home from Cheryl (I give all clients my home number with instructions to call if needed in cases of crisis. It's amazing how carefully they protect my privacy. It's rare when I get called. But, when I do, I know it is important.) Cheryl was crying. I told her I had time to listen and asked her what had happened. She described how that morning, when Ed had just driven off to work, she got a call from one of his subcontractors who told her that he would not be able to make a delivery of asphalt to the job site until early afternoon. He told her that he was unable to get Ed on his cell phone. Would Cheryl let Ed know? Cheryl agreed. She made one call to Ed on his cell phone but got a busy signal. Then she got busy, got the kids ready for their day, got herself ready, went off to work and completely forgot to call Ed. She didn't remember the call until Ed walked in the door after work madder than hell.

"He screamed at me," she said. "He asked me how I could do such a thing. Didn't I know how hard he was working to improve his business?

What kind of wife was I? All this malarkey about being close and moving back into the bedroom was just a set up. He told me I didn't really care. Then he clammed up. Wouldn't talk to me. This infuriated me. I yelled at him. Told him to take his business and shove it. That's all he really cares about anyway. The kids and I don't count, just his damn business. I told him he's depressed but won't get help and I'm doing all the work to keep our relationship together. I told him I'm losing hope and he better come around soon or I wouldn't be there for him when he did. He told me he didn't care. I'm really frustrated, I'm really mad, and I don't know if I want to keep trying anymore."

Cheryl had gotten more of a test than I thought she would. What a terrible fight. Clearly Cheryl was at a crossroads in her work on getting on track.

I told Cheryl I needed to ask a few tough questions. She said that was okay.

"What happened between you and Ed is awful. I'm sure you're feeling miserable and defeated. But that's exactly the kind of marriage you are trying not to have with Ed, the fighting, yelling, withdrawing—the frustration and disappointment. You are not in charge of Ed and what he is like as a husband. You are not in charge of how he reacted when you forgot to tell him about the phone call. I think he overreacted. It's not likely this one incident is going to break the bank. But I'm not in charge of Ed either. What you are in charge of is you. You've gotten off track. Ed has made it very hard to not react. Everybody gets off track. You have. So, let me ask you a question: Do you intend to get a divorce over this incident with Ed? Are you clear you no longer want to be married to Ed?" I asked.

There was a long pause. Finally, Cheryl replied, "No, I'm not going to get a divorce from Ed. But I can't take much more of this. I am feeling defeated. I'm beginning to feel it's not worth it."

"It's okay to feel defeated. You've tried really hard. I admire that. But what you are saying is that you are not planning on getting a divorce from Ed at this time. Then, Cheryl, you are choosing to be married. Ed isn't making you be a wife, you are. I know it's hard to go back to basics at a time like this, but it's important you take charge of yourself. It's the only way you are ever going to be able work your way out of the present situation and ultimately feel good about yourself. Does this make sense so far?" I asked.

"Yeah, I know it does. I know no one can make me be married but me. But it doesn't feel very good. I'm really hurting."

"I know you are hurting. I know it feels awful. I know Ed is hurting, as well. Two people can't yell at each other and withdraw without feeling awful. The second question I want to ask you is this: Are you willing to try to get back on track? You know you are off track as the wife you want to be, independently of what Ed is being like as a husband. I'm not judging you, but trying to help you understand what's going on with you. If you were to try to get back on track where would you start?" I asked.

"Oh boy, you're asking a lot. I know I'm off track but I don't know if I can get back on. It's too hard," Cheryl said.

"I know it's hard. But you and I both know that it will never make sense for you to choose to be married and then stay off track. That's a really hopeless thing to do. That's the marriage that didn't work out, remember? I'm sorry it's so hard," I said.

"I'm sorry too," Cheryl said with a resigned sigh. "But, yes I know, if I choose to be married I should get back on track."

"But where would you start? How will you know if you are getting back on track?"

"Well I'm not going to go in there and get all lovey-dovey as though nothing happened. I'm not going to do that," Cheryl said with determination in her voice.

"Let me suggest something. Expressing your feelings and thoughts is part of what you want to be like as a wife. Also, taking responsibility for your own actions is important—admitting when you are off track. How about telling Ed that you do not like the way he treated you, but that you are sorry for yelling at him—that is not the way you want to treat him no matter whether he yelled at you or not—and apologize for forgetting to call him. Let it go at that. Don't try to engage him in a dialogue about it. Just say your piece. And, then start getting back on track."

"I suppose I could do that. Then I suppose I could look over my list and figure out a place to get started. But I don't feel like it!" Cheryl emphasized.

"I know you don't feel like it. I know how hard this is going to be for you. But I'm very impressed that in the middle of such turmoil you are willing to give it a try. Our next appointment isn't for about a week-and-a-half, so would you call me tomorrow evening and let me know how you did?" I asked.

She thanked me for being available and said she'd really try the things we had talked about. I knew Cheryl would give it her best. She was very determined not to let the old, unsuccessful and hurtful marriage return.

I had asked Cheryl to call me the next day in order to give her all the support I could at this time. This would be her big test. This was the kind of fight that could result in withdrawal from the marriage and eventual divorce. I knew Cheryl loved Ed and wanted the marriage to last. I knew she wanted to feel good about herself as a married woman. In order to do this she would need to know that she could react to Ed, get off track, and then clear her head and get back on. If she could get back on track after this big fight with Ed, I knew her confidence would soar. She would be in charge of her color as a wife like she never had before.

At about 8:00 p.m. the next evening, she called. "This is Cheryl reporting in," she said. "You asked that I call."

"Cheryl you know you don't have to report in to me, but thanks for calling. I've been thinking of your situation, and sending you my best support." I responded.

"I'm just uncomfortable calling you at home," she replied. "But, I do want to thank you for helping me through my fight with Ed last night. I did what we talked about. I got out my list and decided to be responsible for myself. I decided to focus on being caring and pleasant. When I felt I was ready, I went to Ed earlier this evening and told him that I didn't appreciate him yelling at me when he got home. Forgetting to tell him about the business call was an honest mistake. Then I told him I was sorry for yelling at him and putting him down. I told him that that is not what I want to be like as a wife and I apologized for my actions. Then I let it go. Didn't even ask for an explanation. Just said my piece and went back to helping the kids with their homework. Told myself that I had done that pretty well. I knew it wasn't over but I felt better. Then guess what happened?" Cheryl paused. I knew she was teasing me a little bit.

"What," I finally asked.

"About an hour later Ed came up to me and apologized for getting mad at me. He told me it was an honest mistake, that he's forgotten phone calls too. Then he talked about his business and how he feels he takes three steps forward and two back. He said he is making progress and feels more hopeful. He actually shared with me without my asking. Then he told me that he appreciates how hard I've been trying. He said, 'I just wanted to let you know that.' Then out of the blue he tells me he loves me. I haven't heard that in months. Having him tell me he loves me sure helps me get back on track. I can't tell you how good it feels. I learned a lot in the last 24 hours. I can't wait to talk to you about it."

"I'm very glad things are better for you. So, Ed told you he loves you.

SURVIVING SET BACKS

That means a lot; I know it does. Good work, Cheryl. Let's wait for our next appointment to talk about it more, so we have time to explore it better than we can on the phone. Thanks for calling me back. Have a nice evening."

"I will," Cheryl said with confidence.

Cheryl passed her test. She had a fight with Ed, became angry and hurt, reacted to her feelings and got off track, and began feeling hopeless—like it wasn't worth all the effort she had put into being the wife she wants to be. She changed her color from being the wife she wants to be into a dark hue that didn't work for her. Then she became aware that she was off track with herself. That she had reacted to her feelings of hurt and as a result put reactive, temporary feelings in charge of what she was like as a wife. This awareness enabled her to look over her list of action values and formulate a plan for managing her actions as a wife getting back on track. She focused herself on being on track, went to Ed, expressed herself—didn't try to engage him in a debate over what happened—and centered herself on being caring and pleasant. Cheryl got back to the color that worked for her. At our next session, I will try to help Cheryl sort out what she learned from her experience so that she can internalize this knowledge about herself as a married woman for the future.

It was good to see Cheryl at our next session. She was feeling good. I asked her what had happened since I talked with her on the phone.

"A lot happened," she said. "I told you that Ed apologized and we talked about his feelings about his business. Well, we went to bed, cuddled but didn't make love. It wasn't like I was ignoring the fight we had but more like I was getting over it. Like you said once about a boat that makes a wake but keeps going and the wake goes away. The next day I was on track. The more I focused on that, the better I felt. Ed was nicer to me. We even made love one night. I'm feeling closer to him and

I think he is feeling closer to me. I don't think it's completely over—that won't happen until his business is totally back on its feet, but it is certainly better."

It was heartening to see Cheryl begin to experience the benefits of being on track, and how returning to her color as a wife contributed positively to the marital inbetween, thus making it easier for Ed to become more loving.

"Cheryl," I asked, "on a scale of 0 to 10, with 10 being the best the marriage could possibly be and 0 the worst, where would you rate your marriage now?

"About a six," Cheryl said.

"And, where would you have rated it when you first came in?"

"About a one or two, I think."

"So, being married to Ed is feeling pretty good now. That's great. You really tested our idea of what can happen if you get off track and then get back on. That was a terrible fight you and Ed had. Let me ask you some specific questions about what you learned from your experience. For instance, what did you learn by being asked in the midst of your anger and hurt, whether you wanted to be married to Ed?"

"It really challenged me. I could have given up at that point. But really I don't want a divorce. And I know that if I'm not getting a divorce, I'm choosing to be married. It made me aware that I was making a choice and that I'm responsible for my choice. Nobody else is. If I'm going to choose to be married then I better do what I can to make it work. As you've said in the past, nothing else makes sense. Boy is it hard! I sure didn't feel like taking responsibility for my choice to stay married to Ed. I also didn't feel much like admitting my responsibility for failing to let him know about the business call—I was certainly off track in terms of caring about what's important to Ed."

"Okay, so you learned that even in the midst of a fight, in fact, most importantly during a fight, it is necessary to take responsibility for choosing to be married—that this centers you as a wife and sets the stage for getting back on track. I know I may say this too much, but no one can make you be married—it is a choice you make. This is almost like a mantra to me. Once you make the choice then you can connect things to your choice. For instance, you can connect your actions as a wife to the choice you've made to be a married woman, rather than to Ed's behavior as a husband. If you are going to be married, then there is a way you want to be a wife that will work for you. Connecting the way it works for you, to your choice to be married, allows you to take charge of it. For instance, Cheryl, you had a quite a struggle between wanting to really get into being angry and hurt and going in the direction these feelings would dictate, and making yourself act in ways that are true to your values for being a wife. You wanted to strangle Ed, not be pleasant and express yourself. What did you learn from this powerful struggle?"

"Like you have said, no one can make me be married but me. Seeing this as a mantra is probably a good idea. It means I am in charge of me. Ed can make it hard or easy but he's not in charge of what I'm like as a wife. I am. I felt like yelling and screaming and judging and criticizing him because he was acting like a jerk. Well, I'm not in charge of whether he acts like a jerk, I'm only in charge of how I manage myself when he is a jerk. I'm not immune from reacting to him. I'll always have feelings. But I'm learning about these feelings. I'm learning not to let negative feelings dictate the direction I will go as a wife. While I may react, I want it to be temporary, like it was during our fight. Reactive feelings can take me to a marital black hole, and I know that now. It's hard, really hard, to not go there. But when I don't give in to these feelings, I feel really good about myself. I feel strong and capable. Whenever I've let these feelings take over, I've always ended up feeling worse. Then my self-esteem takes a nosedive. It's an awful circle. I'm glad I'm learning to get out of it. I know I will get off track at times. But I know how to center myself and start a process that can get me back on track. If I can do that after a fight like Ed and I had, I know I can really do it. You're right, it was a test," Cheryl said.

"I agree," I said. "If you can center yourself as a wife around the mantra of choosing to be married, while you may temporarily sink into the reactive circle, you will be able to get out of it and back on track. It does feel good to know this and to feel confident that it will help you guide yourself in your marriage. When you went to Ed to tell him how you felt about the way he treated you and the way you responded, you said that you just told him, apologized and then let it go, you didn't try to debate the issues nor discuss them with him. You just said what you had to say. What did you learn from the way you did this?"

"I learned that it is better to express myself and apologize for my part in it and not to debate it. In the past I would have tried to get Ed to agree that he had mistreated me and I never would have apologized for my part. It seemed to me that he was responsible for the way I felt and the way I acted. Now I know that I'm responsible for the way I act. I don't have to try to get Ed to agree with me. I just have to say what I've got to say and let it go at that. That's a real discovery for me. I always thought that we had to talk it out. I didn't know I could just express myself, leave it at that, and then go back to working on being on track. I think the apology was an especially good thing to do. I've never told him I was sorry for what I said and did. I always thought it was his fault. Now I know differently. If I treat him in a way that is inconsistent with my values for being a wife, then I should apologize. My mistreatment comes from my being off track with myself; it's not his doing, it's mine."

"I can't tell you how valuable your insights are, Cheryl. So many couples I've seen get stuck trying to get one another to agree. It's like, 'If I can get him to agree that I'm right, then I can be nice again. But I'm not going to be nice until he sees it my way." Obviously, this doesn't work. What you did does work. Knowing that you can say what's on your mind and let it go at that, and apologize for getting off track with yourself, gives you the power to get unstuck on your own. That's a worthwhile thing to know how to do."

"You are so right. I never knew it could happen the way it did. I really did do a good job, didn't I?" Cheryl stated.

"You bet you did," I said. "So much happened in the incident with Ed. For instance, let me point out something else that can be learned from this. When Ed came home and immediately accused you of screwing up by not remembering to tell him about the phone call, he was allowing himself to be married to you and think negatively about you. I wonder if you do this sometimes. I think we all do as spouses, and it never works. If you are going to choose to be married to Ed, you should always give him the benefit of the doubt—you should always think of him as an adult doing the best he can. For one thing, this positive assumption is probably correct—he probably is doing his best. But most importantly, when you make negative assumptions about Ed, it only makes it harder to be married to him, and especially hard to stay on track. When you make positive assumption, it is more likely true AND it makes it easier to be married to him. Had Ed assumed you were doing your best and in a complex life people forget things and you didn't intentionally try to hurt him, he would have acted differently when he walked in the door. I'm not saying this to criticize Ed, but to point out how the logic applies to you, too. It's not easy to harbor only positive thoughts about your spouse, but it's worth working on."

"I know what you mean," Cheryl said. "When Ed gets into his business and lessens his involvement with me, I assume he's avoiding me. I don't assume he's doing the best he can. If I did assume the best I would feel better about him. I'll check this out. I'll start looking at how I'm thinking about Ed and see if I can't begin thinking more positively about him. Since we made up after the fight, this might be a good place to begin."

MARRIAGE MAKEOVER

STEP ELEVEN

Knowing You Are On Track

*Keeping up the momentum of
being on track with your action values.*

CHERYL PASSED HER MARITAL TEST. She got off track by reacting to Ed, became aware she needed to get back on track and did it. Now if she can keep her "on track" momentum, her marital experience will continue to improve. There are just a couple of things left for us to do and then Cheryl will be on her own.

Cheryl came back to see me in two weeks. She was in a great mood. She reported she was doing a good job of staying on track and felt she and Ed were closer. While the work we were doing was not directed at Ed, I knew that as Cheryl got better at being on track, Ed would change, too. As Cheryl got her best color as a wife going, it automatically became part of the marital inbetween where Ed would experience it. As she became more loving, he experienced her lovingness in the marital inbetween. A normal response to something we experience as positive, is to be positive in return. This is what happened to Ed—he began to experience the positive nature of the action values Cheryl was putting into the marital inbetween, and he responded. Not surprisingly, as Cheryl got on track being pleasant, Ed became more pleasant. Ed's softening became a nice indirect result of Cheryl getting on track. It is worth noting, that marriage would not feel good for Cheryl at this point if she had chosen her action values in order to change Ed. Rather than concentrating on her authenticity, she would have gathered her action values around her in order to change Ed—she would have attempted to become the wife she thought Ed wanted her to be, rather the wife she wanted to be. Deciding what action values to adopt because they can influence your husband and change him, is manipulation of him and abandonment of your selfhood. A marriage built on manipulation and inauthenticity feels hollow and meaningless. Cheryl must be on track as the wife she wants to be in order to feel that being a wife and being married has meaning for her. Marriage would ultimately have no meaning for her if she chose action values for their impact on Ed. She would be married through him and giving herself up exclusively to what she thinks he wants. Her choice to be married would fundamentally change and become centered in Ed. "I'm choosing to be a wife so that I can change my husband and if he changes I must be doing a good job as a wife," would become her paradigm as a married woman. There is nothing wrong with doing things that please your husband, but the focus of your actions for doing what pleases him, must reside in the adoption of action values true to who you want to be as a wife. Happily, Cheryl did adopt action values real to her, and not for the purpose of manipulating Ed. That Ed responded in pleasant ways, turned out to be a nice indirect result of Cheryl being on track. Her actions and his responses felt real. It was nice seeing Cheryl feeling good about herself in her marriage.

We agreed to rate her action values at this time to see how she had been doing and to define any problems that remain to be worked on. Here is how Cheryl's rating turned out.

CHERYL RATES HER ACTION VALUES

Loving	+2	Caring	+1
Faithful	+3	Positive	+2
Light Hearted	+2	Up beat	+2
Sensitive	+2	Attentive	+2
Trusting	+2	Accepting	+2
Assertive	+2	Express Feelings and thoughts	+2
Open	+2	Good Listener	+2
Active	+2	Open minded	+2
Understanding	+3	Affectionate	+2
Sexual	+1	A good lover	+1
Intimate	+1	Sexy	+1
Romantic	+1	Honest	+3
Trustworthy	+3	Balance of individual and shared activities	+1
Polite	+3	Respectful	+3
Even tempered	+2	Share in household tasks	+3
Drug free	+3	Light social drinker	+3
Healthy	+2	Non-judgmental	+2
Nice looking	+2	A good person	+3
Friend	+3	Companion	+2

Based on Cheryl's rating it was not surprising she felt good about herself as a married woman and better about her marriage with Ed. She was on track with herself as the wife she wanted to be. She was managing her wife sphere well. She had a good hold on her wife color.

"Cheryl, you've done a good job. You've gotten yourself on track as the wife you want to be. How does it feel?" I asked.

"I feel so much better, not only about myself but about my marriage, too. I think I'm beginning to understand how marriage works and how to do it. I don't think I ever had really given it much thought. Now that I look back I think I was just too trusting of instincts. Who knows where they come from? But now I feel more like an adult woman. I'm more in charge of me than I ever thought possible. I know it's not over yet. I'll probably be working at staying on track and getting better at it, the rest of my life. But, I know how to do it, thanks to you."

"You're welcome. Thanks for working so hard. We're obviously getting to where you won't need to see me anymore. That's good, although I'll miss you. Before we stop, let's do one more thing that I think will help. Let's fine-tune your list of action values. I don't think it needs to be so long. A lot of the values are similar. Let's go through it and whittle it down to a more workable size. Okay?" I asked.

We went over Cheryl's list, eliminating some action values and keeping others. This was Cheryl's final list: loving, faithful, positive, trusting, accepting, expressing feelings and thoughts, being a good listener, affectionate, sexual, romantic, respectful, and a friend. Cheryl added one new one to her list. She decided she wanted to be nice. She said to me, "You said one time that the hard part of being married is being nice when you don't feel like it. I've always remembered that. It stuck with me. There is a lot of mileage in being nice." So we added it to her list.

Cheryl now has her lifelong list for who she wants to be as a married woman. It's her palette of colors as a wife. Combined, it is her wife color. She is in charge of it and responsible for maintaining it, or for changing it as her sense of who she wants to be evolves.

I saw Cheryl one more time. She said, "Well, Doc, what's next?"

"I think you should go for six months and then call me. We'll talk a little on the phone just to see how you are doing. If you are doing well at staying on track, we'll call it a job well done. I'm really proud of what you have done, Cheryl. I like what you know and how well you are doing. I see the pride and confidence you feel. I wish you the best in your marriage to Ed. I hope I get to meet him someday. He sounds like an honest and hardworking man and a deeply feeling person as well."

"Thank you. I know you would like Ed, if you met him." she said.

Cheryl had come a long way in the six months she worked on her marriage with me. She had overcome her troubled marriage. She no longer felt frustrated, angry and bewildered about her marriage. She was oriented as a reasonable and rationally committed woman, and on track with her action values. Her hard work, perseverance, and belief in herself paid off. She was feeling good about herself in her marriage with Ed and hopeful about the future. Cheryl had recaptured her dreams for a successful marital experience, and it was very heartening for me to see her do so.

What's next for Cheryl is to continue to stay on track over time and in all marital situations, so that greater feelings of satisfaction can occur. Her job is to get better and better at being on track. As Cheryl does this she will begin to attain self-actualization—the self-awareness that she is expressing the best of her human qualities as a married woman—and, as she does this, she will experience more and more fulfillment as a wife.

PART FIVE: MARITAL TIPS

You know that staying on track can be difficult. In the everyday mix of marital life, you will say and do things that upset your husband and he will say and do things that upset you. The more helpful ideas you have for staying on track, the better you will be at it. What follows is a description of helpful hints that I have learned from hundreds of couples who have explored how to stay on track in their marriage. Included also are ideas for increasing your fulfillment as a wife. I think these tips have tremendous value and can help you stay on track and achieve greater satisfaction as a spouse.

MARRIAGE MAKEOVER
STEP TWELVE

De-Escalating Arguments

*How to prevent arguments
from getting out of control.*

WHAT DO YOU DO WHEN YOUR HUSBAND says or does something that really irritates, angers, frustrates and hurts you AND you are about to lose it? You feel yourself ready to explode. You are going to get off track in a big way, and you know you won't like yourself afterwards. As they say, "Been there, done that." The answer is learning some skills that have great po-

DE-ESCALATING ARGUMENTS

tential in situations where you are likely to explode. The first is called "time out."

What is time out? It is not throwing up your hands in frustration and walking out. It is not putting on a demeanor of stony silence. It is not threatening to leave or get a divorce. Time out is an agreed-upon break. It is a recognition that you are about to lose it and rather than add fuel to the fire, it is better to take time out.

Here's how Scott and Melanie, who were about six months into a developing relationship at the time I met them, learned to use time out. Scott is the kind of guy who wants an explanation. He can hardly breathe when faced with unknowns and uncertainties. Melanie is accustomed to lots of time alone. She is accustomed to making her own decisions and not discussing or negotiating them with anyone. When Scott and Melanie met and were seriously attracted to each other, their styles clashed. Awful scenes occurred with Scott wanting to know why Melanie did or did not want to do something and Melanie giving one simple explanation and wanting it to end there. Scott would pursue, and Melanie would back up. When she got really frustrated, Melanie would walk out, go home, and would unplug her phone for the rest of the night. This drove Scott wild with apprehension. These scenes were threatening to break up an otherwise terrific relationship, because when they were not creating these scenes, they really liked each other very much. They shared an interest in cooking and movies and got along great most of the time. Their promising relationship, however, was doomed to break up until they learned how to do time outs.

The rules they agreed upon for time out were simple. (1) Melanie will monitor her frustration level on a scale of 0 to 10. (2) When it reached a five she will call time out. She will say out loud, "time out." (3) She will tell Scott how much time she would take, say 30 minutes. (4) Scott agrees to honor her request for time out no matter how frustrated he might feel. He will put himself into a holding pattern. He will not pursue her. (5) When the time is up, Melanie will come back to Scott and reinitiate conversation about the subject they had been talking about. They both agree that whomever initiated the time out will take responsibility for coming back to renew interaction. (6) Each agreed to stay on track while talking about the issues.

They practiced time outs. They treated time outs as a skill to learn. They got good at doing it. As a result of using time outs, their positive interaction remained the same, while their negative interactions decreased. Moreover, by using time outs they entirely cut out the awful moments of frustration and apprehension caused by stormy and threatening separations. Today, Melanie and Scott are married. They may not have made it to the altar had they not learned to take time outs. This was a big payoff for a relatively easy effort.

Staying on track is the ultimate purpose of using time out. When you know you are about to lose control of your "on-trackness," instead of exploding, you call time out. You take a break, get calm, remind yourself of your action values, go back to your husband and renew discussion of the subject at hand. If you are on track, you can talk about anything. If you are off track, no matter what you try to talk about, it is very likely to turn out badly. Time outs can be an essential tool for helping you stay on track.

Using time out works best when both you and your husband agree to the rules of time out. Both of you agree to honor the request for time out under all circumstances. In sports, for instance, it is agreed that if a participant calls a time out, it is immediately granted. Even a hand signal is agreed upon in advance as a way of indicating the calling of a time out period, and the duration is preset. Everybody honors the time out. When the time has elapsed, everyone goes back to playing the game. Men and women who have played sports or who are sports fans know this.

DE-ESCALATING ARGUMENTS

If you believe using time out will be helpful to you in your attempt to stay on track in your marriage, talk it over with your husband. Remind him how the concept is used in sports. Ask him what would happen in sports if time out requests were not honored. Ask him if he would be willing to adopt the use of time outs in your marriage. If you are both sports-minded, agree to use the sports hand signal for calling time out. This signal is already embedded in your "sports mind," so a reflex to honor it is ready made. You might even consider having fun practicing time outs in another way. I know a couple who were learning to use time outs and she called for one in the middle of sex. They both froze for a few seconds and got a good giggle out of the experience. The more you practice time outs in non-threatening situations, the more likely the skill will be there for you when you need it most.

While time out works best when both you and your husband agree to its use, it can be done even if your husband does not agree to it. If you have a husband who says, "No way. It's stupid. I'm not going to do it," you can still use time out in your own way. In domestic violence programs, the offender is taught that he (sometimes it is a she) is responsible for avoiding situations where he is abusive. The offender is taught to use time out. He is told that he is fully responsible for avoiding situations where he might be abusive. He is taught to monitor his "emotional temperature" on a scale of 0-10, and when it reaches a five, to announce that he is taking a time out for 30 minutes. No matter what his wife does, he is taught that it is his responsibility to leave the situation immediately. If his wife follows him as he attempts to leave, he is to do whatever necessary and non-violent to exit the situation. If he has to lock himself in the bathroom, telling his wife through the door that he is taking time out, to please leave him alone for awhile, if he has to leave the house for a drive, whatever he needs to do to leave the situation, he must do it to prevent himself from becoming abusive. After he has regained control of his anger, cooled himself down, and within the prescribed time limit, he goes back to his wife with a willingness to talk about the issue they had been discussing. If his emotional temperature goes beyond a five again, once more he must take time out. He does this every time it is needed to avoid becoming abusive to his wife. Obviously, over time, the use of time out becomes easier, eventually settling into an accepted routine by both spouses.

If you are unable to obtain an agreement to the mutual use of time out with your husband, you can employ the procedure outlined above. Keep in mind, the purpose of time out is to prevent you from getting off track. It serves your purposes to avoid situations that may result in your escalating out of control and getting seriously off track. Time out is effective and worth introducing into your repertoire of wisdom and skill as a married woman. Whether you take time out as a mutually agreed upon decision with your spouse, or on your own, it can be invaluable in helping you stay on track.

MARRIAGE MAKEOVER

STEP THIRTEEN

How to Apologize

The essence of a self-respecting apology.

HOW DO YOU KNOW WHEN TO APOLOGIZE? What's the best reason for saying you are sorry, and what do you say when you do it?

Inevitably, you are not always going to be the married woman you want to be. No matter how hard you try, how long you work at it, or how good you get at it, you will get off track from time to time. This is the case for everyone. Of course, there are big ways to get off track, like walking out, calling names, threatening divorce, yelling, or throwing things! And then, there are little ways of getting off track, such as withholding what's on your mind, failing to be polite, indulging negative thoughts about your spouse, and so on. No matter whether it is big or little, you won't feel delighted with yourself as a wife if you experience conflict between your values and your actions. Thus, when you treat your husband differently than the way you want to treat him because you have been off track, you should apologize.

Whenever you get off track from the way you want to be as a spouse, and as a result mistreat your husband according to the standards you have set for yourself as a married woman, you should tell him you are sorry. You don't necessarily apologize because he is hurt or unhappy—although that can be part of it—but because of the way you treated him. You are sorry because that's not the way YOU want to treat him. You're sorry for mistreating him, and you're sorry for hurting him.

If you are out to dinner with friends and later he says in reference to something you said at the dinner table, "that was not a very nice way to talk to me in front our friends. It seemed like you were belittling me. I felt pretty put down by what you said," and you look inside yourself and conclude that indeed you had been dismissive in front of friends, then you apologize. Putting him down is not on your list of action values. In the case of Cheryl, being kind, supportive, and positive are on her action value list. So, if she were to act in belittling ways as a wife, she would be off track. She would apologize.

Perhaps you listed values similar to Cheryl's. If so, you would apologize. You'd say, "I'm sorry. That's not the way I want to treat you. I'm sorry I was critical. I'm sorry if I hurt you." In other words, you apologize for your actions and acknowledge the fact that you were not behaving in accord with values that you hold to be deeply important to you, and as a result inflicted hurt on your husband.

What if your husband does not accept your apology? What if he brushes it off as insincere or simply remains silent, thus withholding confirmation of your expression of regret? Do not be overly concerned with whether your husband accepts your apology or not. You are not in charge of whether he accepts it or not, that is his territory. You are only in charge of whether or not you have acted in line with your values for how you want to treat him and, when you have gotten off track, for apologizing. Focus on the fact that you have rightly apologized, not on whether he accepts it. You did your part. After apologizing, focus on being on track. If he continues to be hurt or angry, stick with your action values. That's the most you can do about it. By remaining consistent to your own values, you will end up contributing to a marital inbetween that gives him the best chance of resolving his feelings with you. You are not taking care of him and his hurt feelings, you are bringing to the marital inbetween your best participation. This is you doing your part to help build a pathway out of the hurt or anger. If you remain loving, positive, respectful, and good-natured you will have done your part. When you've apologized and realigned yourself with your finest characteristics of who you want to be, what more can you do?

What if he complains about the way you treated him, but you don't agree? Then you still stay on track and act kindly and supportively (if these are your values) and say, "I'm sorry you feel badly about the way I treated you." You acknowledge his feelings and let it go at that. He's a strong, adult male. He can resolve feelings. Stay on track and let him do it.

What if he thinks you should apologize but you don't? You take an honest look at your actions and your values, and you conclude, "I don't think I behaved badly. I think I was on track." You know he thinks you've hurt him. His feelings tell him something happened and he blames you. Some psychologists tell us not to sweat the small stuff. This is an example. This is a small matter because it is easy to resolve. Now, it can become a big deal if you decide to argue that point: "I did nothing to hurt you. It's all in your mind. Don't take it out on me." Why go this direction? Why not just say, "I'm sorry your feelings are hurt. I didn't intend to hurt you, and if I've inadvertently upset you, I'm sorry." You've spoken the truth: you didn't set out to hurt him by your actions. Let it go at this. Chances are this will disarm the situation, bring it to an end, and allow you both to go on with your evening unencumbered with negative emotions.

MARRIAGE MAKEOVER

STEP FOURTEEN

Overcoming the Fear You Will Upset Him

The rule "don't dodge it."

THERE MAY BE TIMES AS A WIFE when you think, "If I tell my husband what I'm thinking, he'll get upset, so, I'd better not say anything and just make the best of it." When this dilemma presents itself, it is easy to get confused and silently withdraw. A married woman can find herself protecting a (adult) husband from feelings she thinks he can't handle and protecting herself from conflict she thinks she can't handle. Thinking your husband will get upset and that this must be avoided, does not work, so don't let it happen to you! The focus needs to shift away from what his reaction may be, to the unworkable direction you are taking in your communication with him.

Many wives go to great lengths to avoid conflict. These women "mind read" their husband and think, "If I say what's on my mind, he will get upset. If I tell him to drive more slowly, to stop smoking, to drink less, to visit his parents more often, to stop swearing so much around the kids, to be more gentle in sex, etc., he will get upset or his feelings will be hurt." These wives act as though the rule is "don't do anything that upsets or hurts your husband's feelings."

OVERCOMING THE FEAR YOU WILL UPSET HIM

It doesn't work to avoid saying what is bothering you because you believe it will upset your husband. You can't have a successful marriage if you imagine conflict will occur if you speak up. It doesn't work that way and you know it. Side-stepping communication doesn't work, but the "don't dodge it" rule does.

The rule of "don't dodge it" means that if something is important to you and *you think by bringing it up your husband will be upset,* you *have to* bring it up. That's right; have to! Here is how the rule works:

It doesn't matter so much specifically what's on your mind. What matters is that you are thinking that if you speak up he'll get upset and therefore you set aside your own thoughts and feelings to avoid conflict. You are presenting an internal argument to yourself that will censor what you want to say. Remember, if you are on track, you can talk about anything and communication is likely to be productive. Thus, your problem is one of staying on track and saying what you want to say and not a problem of whether it will upset your husband. Make it a rule for yourself as a married woman that if you find yourself thinking that what you want to say may upset your husband (and you feel yourself holding back because it *may* upset him) then you have to say what's on your mind. It's the best thing to do. Of course, if violence is what you anticipate from him, the problem is not going to be solved by provoking him. You need to deal with whether you will remain married to an abusive, violence prone husband.

Whether he'll be upset is not the deciding point for when you should edit yourself. He's an adult, he can handle upsets—it is not your job to protect him from your important thoughts and feelings. It is your job to say what is on your mind and to be fully aligned with your own values as you say it. Many times in a marriage, trying to avoid conflict by ignoring or setting aside thoughts and feelings creates a worse marital dynamic in the long run, than differences caused by a truthful and on track expression of opinion.

Many women struggle with this rule. The married women I have known who have stopped censoring and started expressing, tell me they prefer it over worrying about upsetting their husbands. As an example, for years Leah had withheld her opinions if she thought expressing them would upset her husband, Steve. She walked on eggshells, treading a fine line between what she thought, what she wanted to say, and what she thought might upset Steve. Steve's reactions weren't any help, either. He was like a little boy at times, losing his temper if he didn't get his way, objecting in critical terms to issues over which he and Leah disagreed. He was moody and discontented a lot of the time, complaining about life's circumstances. Keeping him from getting upset felt like a full time job to Leah. When she heard about the rule, "don't dodge it," she decided to stop censoring herself on the basis of whether she thought it would upset Steve. She did the hard work of getting on track and then began expressing herself. She was kind and thoughtful and became open and expressive as well. When she began to express herself and not hold back because she thought Steve would get upset, Steve went into a tailspin. It seemed he reacted by being angry and sullen most of time. He was miserable. He began to experience sleep and appetite disturbances. His concentration and memory deteriorated. He was having a bad time. Still, Leah stuck by her guns. She knew she was doing nothing wrong and it was better in the long run for her to express herself in her marriage than to stuff her thoughts and feelings because Steve got upset. Finally, Steve felt bad enough to disclose to a good friend what he had been going through. His friend told him about a men's group he had been going to and how it helped him understand the relationship between feelings of dependency and anger. Steve was skeptical at first but decided to give it a try. Within a few weeks he felt better. His moods leveled out. He had greater resiliency to deal with difficulties and differences around him. He became more settled and sure of himself than he had ever been in Leah's memory with him. She liked these changes. She continued to express herself openly and without fear Steve would get upset. In fact, Steve rarely got upset but interacted with her in an even and considerate manner.

Steve had been stuck in a syndrome of dependency-generated anger for years. Leah's attempt to compensate for his moods by trying not to upset him was part of what made it possible for him to continue being stuck. It was tolerable, but not okay. When Leah opened up, Steve's mood worsened and an opportunity came along to take care of a problem he had ignored for years. Steve's problem was solvable. When he went to the men's group and began to understand the dynamics around his angry mood, he got better. Leah and Steve could have gone along for years doing a dissatisfying and unworkable dance around his moodiness, and Steve never would have figured out his problem, if Leah had not gotten on track and begun following the rule of "don't dodge it." By introducing the rule, "don't dodge it," Leah stopped hiding her opinions and brought an open and expressive dimension to her marriage with Steve, and a long ignored problem got successfully addressed. Whatever is going on in your marriage that concerns you, avoiding the issue because it may upset your husband will not work. It's better to speak up and see where it leads you than to allow a stifling dynamic rule your marital interactions. Leah stopped hiding behind her fears and experienced the benefits in her marriage by the rule "don't dodge it."

Let me describe a really powerful issue that Mike and Beth discussed so that you can see how the "rule" works in very difficult circumstances. Beth didn't want to have children. She liked her career, her marriage, her social world and she didn't feel the need to change any of this by having a child. She did not feel strong maternal yearnings. On the other hand, she knew Mike wanted a child. She often heard him talk about it to his parents and friends. She was afraid that if she told Mike she didn't want a child, he would get upset and she even feared he might want to get a divorce. When Mike would bring up the desire for her to get pregnant and talk about having a child, Beth would remain silent and look for opportunities to change the subject. After thinking about her differences with Mike on the subject, Beth decided she had to bring it up. Withholding her opinion was not a good long-term strategy for being married and it was inconsistent with her marital value to express her feelings and thoughts and be open and honest.

Beth got up her courage and one night after dinner said to Mike, "I have something really important I want to talk to you about. Is this a good time?" Mike nodded "yes." Beth said, "This is really hard for me. I love you and want to be with your forever, but I'm afraid you'll get upset and angry at me if I tell you—that you might not want to be married to me anymore. I know you've always wanted to have a child. I hear you talk about it to your parents and I see the way you look at little kids. With both of us reaching our mid-thirties, people are beginning to wonder, and some have even asked if we're planning a family. You have a lot of love to give a child and I feel really terrible, but I don't want to have a child and I don't think I ever will. I like my career, I like my life and I love being married to you, but I've thought a lot about it and I'm really clear now. I know I don't want to. I just honestly don't want a child. I'm truly sorry if this hurts you." Beth got a lot off her mind and did a good job of being on track in the way she expressed herself.

Mike's first reaction was just what Beth had feared. He was angry, confused and hurt. He accused Beth of hiding her true feelings from him. He brought up questions of whether he could ever trust her entirely again. For several days, Mike withdrew and had only functional communication with Beth. When Mike did open up and talk about his anger and hurt, Beth listened, explained, and listened some more. She remained clear about not wanting to have children. Mike remained adamant that he wanted children and in saying he felt Beth had deceived him.

Because the possibility of a happy resolution to this conflict seemed unlikely, Beth had second thoughts. She feared she had done the wrong thing in telling Mike. The thought that he might divorce her sent shudders through her heart, but she held her ground and stayed on track. She consistently made an effort not to react to Mike's anger and blame but rather to understand that he was deeply hurt. Mike alternated between deep confusion and flickers of understanding and acceptance. He had gotten married with the assumption in his mind that they would eventually have a family. It's what he wanted. The psychological distance from the assumption that he would have a child, to accepting he would not be a father was enormous for him.

Beth made herself available at any time to listen to him and talk more about her thoughts and feelings. As time progressed, Beth and Mike's marital actions focused on talking about his hurt and her guilt. Their emotional distance lessened. Beth became hopeful her marriage with Mike would survive.

Finally, Mike's anger and blame lessened and it became apparent his actual response to Beth's announcement was hurt and disappointment rather than the anger that appeared on the surface. Beth was able to respond to his hurt feelings. She listened, she reassured him that she loved him and wanted to remain married to him. As Mike's hurt and disappointment became more manageable, Beth and Mike began wondering about other ways Mike could get his need for children met. This led to a creative stage of communication that Beth never knew they could do. Their energy began to shift from expressions of dismay to ideas about solutions. After several weeks, Beth and Mike reached an understanding. Mike decided to stay married to Beth but he wanted more. He decided to see what he could do in his community to become more involved with children. If this turned out to fulfill his needs for a parental, protective and leadership-type role in the life of a child, Mike said he would be okay and their marriage would continue. If it didn't, then he and Beth would talk about whether to have children or not and what their decision meant about staying married, or getting a divorce. While Beth would have liked a stronger commitment to their marriage than this, she was relieved to begin moving in a direction that *might* lead to remaining married.

Mike made a sincere and creative effort to seek involvement with children in his community. He joined a community organization and became a Big Brother. He volunteered to help coach a soccer team for boys and girls. He became an assistant Cub Scout leader. He brought his "little brother" home for visits, had soccer team parties at his house, and hosted some Cub Scout meetings at home. While this didn't completely fulfill his desire for children of his own, it provided him loads of satisfaction in a parent-like way. He felt he was making a difference in the lives of children.

Beth felt hopeful. Her guilt lessened significantly. She had never felt so emotionally close to Mike. She was glad she had brought up the issue of not wanting to have a child. In looking back, Beth knew that if she hadn't brought it up but had passively hoped the issue would go away, that she would have wounded the marriage, perhaps fatally. By following the rule of "don't dodge it," she had given open communication a chance to resolve an important issue.

Other married women have also learned the importance of the rule, as well. Ruth had never particularly liked the house she and Les lived in. It was his house when they married and she never felt as much as an equal in it as she would have wanted. She always thought if she brought up her feelings and thoughts about the house, Les would get upset. When she learned about the rule "don't dodge it!", she decided to try it. Much to her surprise, when she told Les how she felt about the house and of her desire to buy a new house, he agreed. Just like that! He thought it was a good idea. He believed it would be good for them to have a house they both bought and owned. Ruth was startled by his favorable response. She became a big believer in the idea of self-expression. She dismayed that she had swallowed her thoughts for so long. No more, she promised herself.

Mary Ann was really tired of cutting her husband's hair. At first it had felt like an intimate sharing event between them. After months and years, it had become a chore. She had always feared that if she told Eric how she felt, he would be angry. When she read about the rule "don't dodge it," she decided to tell Eric that she didn't want to do cut his hair anymore. Eric hit the roof. He angrily told her she was being selfish and then he listed all the things he was doing for her. Mary Ann was taken back by the intensity of Eric's feelings. "Maybe I should have kept my mouth shut," she thought. But, the cat was out of the bag anyway, so why not follow through and see where her honesty would lead? She knew it was not a divorce issue. The marriage wasn't threatened by her desire to no longer cut Eric's hair.

After the initial storm, Mary Ann got creative. She asked a few of Eric's friends where they got their haircut. She went to a couple of these places and got Eric gift certificates for two haircuts at each place. She created a present by wrapping the gift certificates along with a new woodworking tool—Eric was a part-time furniture maker—and gave them to her husband. At first Eric scoffed at the certificates. Then Mary Ann told him that his friend Tom went to one of the places for his haircuts and that Dan went to the other. She said, "Why not try it, what do you have to lose?" The matter was dropped. Mary Ann waited to see what Eric would do. About a week later, on a Saturday, Eric came home with his haircut. He didn't say anything and Mary Ann didn't either. Three weeks later, Eric came home with his hair cut again. Neither said anything. Then one day, both Tom and Dan were over, and in front of Mary Ann, they told Eric that his hair looked good and kidded him that Mary Ann probably thought he was a pretty sexy guy again. Everybody had a good laugh. Mary Ann went over to Eric and ruffled his hair and said, "Yeah, he's a hunk." Later, she told Eric she appreciated his efforts to give her a break on cutting his hair and that she wouldn't mind doing it once in a while. He told Mary Ann he liked her cutting his hair and appreciated her not wanting it to become a chore. He told her to let him know if she didn't want to do it and he would go to the barber.

As a consequence of Mary Ann's efforts to open her feelings and thoughts about cutting Eric's hair, she and Eric solved a problem and created greater confidence in their communication with one another. She also processed her own resentment about the hair cutting, and discovered that she doesn't mind doing an occasional trim. In fact, cutting his hair regained some of the close feelings it had for her when she first began doing it. Now, Mary Ann is a believer in the rule, "don't dodge it."

No matter what the issue, if it is bothering you and *you think by bringing it up your husband will get upset*—bring it up! Make this a rule for yourself as a married woman. Put the rule in your mind and believe in it. Practice it. Get good at it.

You may be wondering if you should tell your husband everything that bothers you. No. That's not the rule. Mary Ann, for instance, could have thought, "I'm really tired of cutting Eric's hair. It's not fun anymore. But, he does a lot of things for me that he doesn't complain about. I know he likes me to cut his hair. I appreciate things he does for me and he doesn't complain." Mary Ann could have decided to continue to cut Eric's hair and not to say anything about it. The difference between

OVERCOMING THE FEAR YOU WILL UPSET HIM

Mary Ann's decision to continue to cut her husband's hair and not say anything, is she doesn't think he will get upset and she doesn't use this thought as a basis of self-censorship. Mary Ann has a right to make a choice of whether or not to cut Eric's hair and whether or not to speak up about it—a married woman always has the right to decide whether to express her opinion or not—but stuffing her feelings and thoughts because she thinks bringing them up will upset her husband is not a good marital reason to keep quiet.

Looking at your thoughts in the light of the rule "don't dodge it" can help you decide whether to speak up. Being successfully married does not include withholding your feelings and thoughts because they may upset your husband.

MARRIAGE MAKEOVER

STEP FIFTEEN

Actions Speak Louder than Words

*How to use the quiet power
of being on track to resolve resentments.*

No matter to whom you are married, you will have conflicts. Inevitably, your husband will do something that hurts your feelings. You will do something that hurts his feelings. You will have differences and you will not like it and you will want to resolve them and make up. We have already seen how staying on track can help you resolve your anger and hurt. But when do you rely on the talking part of staying on track and when do you switch to the action part of staying on track to resolve hurt and angry feelings? Some wives (and husbands) seem to want to talk about everything. They act out the logic that talking is the best way to resolve all hurt feelings. Actually, a better rule is to rely on actions as a first priority to get over anger or hurt feelings and to use talk if actions don't work. I know this rule runs counter to much in the self help literature—and what many women feel is common sense—that you have to talk about it. Try what I am suggesting and see what you think. Here is an example of how it can work:

You and your husband have friends over for dinner. During dinner conversation, your husband asks you a question. You address his question as part of the flow of conversation, but he asks you the same question again. You answer it. He looks annoyed. Apparently, he feels you talked but did not answer his question. He says in a demanding and unkind voice, "For Christ sake, will you just answer my question?" Dinner conversation comes to a halt. You look at him and he looks at you. You can see his awareness click on as he thinks, "Oh my, that was a harsh way of putting it." You think to yourself, "I'm not going to react to the way he talked to me. He's making it hard, but I'm going to stay on track." You ask your guests if anyone wants more wine and you refill their glasses. You ask your husband if he would like some and he says yes. You refill his glass. Dinner conversation resumes as everyone moves past the incident. Your husband, who is a nice guy by nature—his outburst was out of character—returns to his usual self: he's nice, attentive, and caring towards you. It's not a ploy but a genuine expression of how he feels about you. You never got off track so you continue on with being nice, attentive and thoughtful toward him. Good will is reestablished between you and your husband. You love him and he loves you, and it shows.

When the evening is over, you feel no animosity toward your husband. Your heart is okay. Your former reaction would be to talk about it, but the incident feels over. No denial, just a resolved sense of resolution. You and your husband made up through your actions of staying on track. When your husband behaved unkindly, you didn't react by getting off track. By staying on track you created a climate which made it easier for him to recover his composure, and easier for you both to get over the temporary setback. If either of you had traded negative reactions, his outburst could have resulted in a nagging resentment that could take on a life of its own, needing further work in order for resolution to occur. As it was, you were both over it and didn't need to talk about it.

The best way to get over hurt and angry feelings is stay on track and find out what happens to your feelings. Chances are you and your husband will make up as a by-product of staying on track. You will resolve hurt or angry feelings by maintaining action values that allow for positive feelings to replace the negative ones. You will move through the negative feelings. You will feel better because you introduced into your marital inbetween, feelings of caring. You will have made up in your heart—the feeling part of you—where it counts.

Married women who try this tell me it is very hard to do at first. They feel compelled to talk about "it." They struggle to release themselves from the injunction "it has to be talked about for me to get over it." However, once they are able to stay on track and can see where that leads them, they tell me it works. In fact, it feels a little too easy. At first, they are suspicious of the outcome—"Am I being genuine, is it real?"—but they soon discover it is. Their emotional calm confirms the resolution is real. They like the results. They discover they haven't given up the talking pathway to conflict resolution, they have just begun to use it where it works best. If, by staying on track, a wife does not feel an issue between her and her husband is resolved, she can then use talk to resolve it. That's where talk works best—after you have gotten back on track—but when getting back on track has not been enough by itself to reach resolution. Then, by combining actions that express your own values with heartfelt talk, a resolution can be attempted. You haven't given up anything by relying on actions first, you have simply prioritized and added to your repertoire another useful pathway toward resolution.

See what you find out by first relying on the quiet power of those action values you have already identified and committed yourself to, to resolve negative feelings. Don't give up on the power of talk, but prioritize talk as the second pathway to resolution, not the first.

MARRIAGE MAKEOVER
STEP SIXTEEN

Deciding Household Tasks

How to sort out who will do this or that?

IF YOU HAVE BEEN MARRIED FOR LONG, you know how complicated it is to manage household tasks. There are hundreds of things that need doing—the shopping, the cooking, the cleaning, the car maintenance, the animal care, the correspondence, the garden, the finances, the vacations, the illnesses, the shopping, and the child care—all need to be managed. Every marital pair must work out a way to get all of this done. There are three ways couples decide who is going to do what: through attrition; by negotiation; and from acting on what bothers the individual spouse. Most couples work out a blend of all three.

ATTRITION

Attrition you know about. It comes from just letting it happen. Over time you end up with "your" household territory to manage and he ends up with "his." Duties that get assigned through attrition eventually become roles in the marriage. Good or bad, effective or ineffective, roles get established.

Attrition can also result in a comfortable dance with each spouse knowing the steps and fitting with the other quite nicely. The key to telling the difference between an attrition-determined role that works for you and one that doesn't, is in your feelings and the results. If you are comfortable with what you do in the marriage on a regular basis and your husband seems reasonably content as well and what gets done is satisfactory, then you are okay. No resentments, no problem. You are the boss of your life, so if you have no problem with your role, no problem exists. There is no inherent right or wrong role as long as what you do and don't do works well for you and your husband and it feels all right to you.

NEGOTIATION

Marriages are in constant flux. What was a comfortable role for your mother as a married woman, is probably different than the way you want to be a wife in your marriage. Role expectations are changing as men and women define themselves as more diverse and equal. The ethic of "my time and energy and your time and energy are equally valuable," is here. Being a woman does not mean that you must do all the laundry for example. Being a man does not mean your husband must do all the yard work. Gender roles no longer hold the power they used to. Today, negotiation and pragmatism play a larger role in the decision of who does what. Negotiation fits nicely with equality. If a job needs to be done, let's decide who is going to do it.

The equality comes from the fairness of the process, not from the results measured by who does what. More and more, pragmatic negotiation is emerging as the marital ethic affecting decisions about the division of household tasks. For instance, in today's marriages it is not uncommon to hear couples openly talk about who will do what. It is not unusual to hear them say something like this: "I'll (the wife) do the cooking because I'm better at it than you and you do the cleanup. We'll both do the shopping. Nobody should have to cook all the time, so I'll (the husband) be responsible for dinner two nights a week. I'll (the husband) clean and keep the house picked up. I'll (the wife) do the gardening. I'll (the husband) balance the check books and take care of the cars."

These understandings are talked about and settled upon by mutual agreement. You talk about it and decide what each of you will do. Of course, the individual talents and inclinations of a given couple may determine that the wife keeps the books, maintains the vehicles and that the husband does laundry and cooking. The care of children and responsibility for aging parents are fertile grounds for negotiated solutions based upon style, time and substance, as well as the pragmatic question, "What works?"

Negotiation demands openness, understanding, flexibility, dependability and reliability. It is a reasonable and rational adult approach to the division of labor and it works quite well. It can identify most household tasks and who will do them.

TAKING RESPONSIBILITY FOR WHAT BOTHERS YOU

While attrition and negotiation are effective, they will not identify all that needs to be done. So, what can you do about the tasks that cannot be anticipated—those little things needing to be done that crop up unexpectedly? These are best taken care of by taking responsibility and action for what bothers you. For example, you get bugged when the dog begins to shed, or look shaggy. You're bothered so you become the self-appointed dog groomer, or the taxi driver taking the dog for haircuts. Your husband is driven wild when dandelions sprout their plucky yellow blooms in the garden, so he takes responsibility for managing weed control. Taking care of what bothers you will fine-tune your list of what you will do and what he will do. It is a very adult method of divvying up territory by taking into account your own preferences—by making yourself accountable for them. The rule is simple—if it bothers you, take care of it.

If clutter bothers you, pick it up. Not because the cleanup of clutter is on your negotiated list, but because it bothers you. If dirty dishes in the sink bother you, clean them up. If a messy car bothers you, clean it up. If fleas on the pet bother you, shampoo the pet. If a dirty bathtub bothers you, clean it up. If soiled and unkempt clothes bother you, wash and sort them. If unpaid bills bother you, pay them.

There is a history to what specifically bothers you; the feeling doesn't come out of the blue. Your personal history is specific to you and it governs what bothers you. If you are bothered by clutter, it is your personal history that shapes this reflex. "If it bothers you, take care of it," is a simple rule that allows you to act on your own initiative and leads to a reduction in what bothers you. Lessening what bothers you on your own leads to less frustration than trying to get your husband to take care of something because it may be on his list, but bothers you more than it bothers him. Trudy found this out when she got tired of reminding her husband, Neil, to clean the kitchen floor. Cleaning the kitchen floor was on Neil's list. He got around to it about every four weeks. Trudy felt herself become irritated with the "dirty" kitchen floor after only a week. She tried reminding Neil and she tried ignoring her irritation. Neither worked well.

Finally, Trudy asked Neil how he felt about cleaning the kitchen floor. He said he didn't mind doing it and thought if it was done about every three to four weeks and that would be satisfactory. As Trudy listened, she discovered that a dirty kitchen floor bothered her before it bothered him. She was bothered in a week and he was bothered in about four weeks. Trudy was trying to get him to clean it when it bothered her and

DECIDING HOUSEHOLD TASKS

before it bothered him. She asked him if he had any gripes about household tasks that she did. He said, "yeah, you don't put things back and clutter builds up and then I end up taking care of it. I'm always picking up and straightening and cleaning countertops and tables." Applying the principle of being bothered, she heard Neil say that he was bothered by clutter before she was, so he was doing it because it bothered him. Trudy and Neil made a deal. Trudy would clean the kitchen floor and Neil would pick up and straighten up clutter. She would take care of what bothered her and he would take care of what bothered him. By talking about and taking responsibility for what bothered them, they modified their negotiated list of household tasks, and came up with a better fit. And, because she agreed to take on a task—the kitchen floor—that bothered her and he agreed to take care of a task—clutter—that bothered him, these tasks acquired a greater probability of getting done on a regular and timely basis.

When the allocation of tasks is done by the principles of attrition, negotiation, and taking care of what bothers you, a really effective system emerges for jointly getting household tasks done.

At first, some wives express apprehension that they will be taking care of everything. Nothing bothers my husband, they say. This is simply not true. Watch him and what he does around the house and you will notice that his movements or complaints are governed by what bothers him. Either he is taking care of things or he is trying to get you to take care of things that bother him. He is bothered by particular household tasks not getting done. Watch, listen and apply the notion of being bothered. Notice what gets done and what doesn't, and who is bothered and who isn't, and you will acquire a base from which household tasks can be pragmatically negotiated and allocated. In the extreme case where you have a husband who truly does nothing and refuses to negotiate, you may have serious problems to address in the relationship, or perhaps a condition for continuing in your marriage.

In Part Six, under the heading, "Obsessive-Compulsive Personality Disorder," I will describe a more severe problem concerning household tasks, one that requires treatment to resolve. While most household tasks can be sorted out between a wife and husband through attrition, negotiation, and acting on what bothers you, an obsessive-compulsive disorder cannot, as you will see.

MARRIAGE MAKEOVER

STEP SEVENTEEN

Supporting Individual Differences

*Your husband has his interests
and you have yours. That's okay.*

WHAT SHOULD YOU DO when your husband tells you he wants to do something that really interests him but is outside the expectations of the marriage you want? What he wants to do is not threatening to the basic structure of the marriage—he doesn't want to start having sex with other women, or live separately—but more an activity of personal interest to him. Because what he wants to do is outside usual expectations, it may stir up uncertainties and insecurities in you. For instance, Bob came to his wife, Wendy and told her that he wanted to get a super streetcar and start drag racing. Wendy didn't even know what a "super street car" was, but thought it was kind of a cute name. When he told her a super streetcar could reach speeds up to 165mph and travel 1/4 mile from a standing start in about 8 seconds, she was flabbergasted. "I don't want my husband on a drag strip, or anywhere else driving at speeds like that," she thought. This hobby sounded dangerous to her. Immediately her mind filled with images of Bob carried off on a stretcher either crippled for life or fatally injured. Bob had done some drag racing before he met Wendy and he had it all figured out: the costs, the time, the team, the ways the whole family could participate—he was really excited. He explained that drag racing wasn't what it used to be, with idiots out there seeing how fast they could go at any cost. Drag racing had become a safe sport with lots of families joining in, he explained.

What approach did Wendy take to Bob's idea? Did she say "no way"? Did she tell him it would take him away from the family too much? Did she tell him it would be a burden on her and the kids? Did she get into how they could not afford it? Wendy had a choice to make about how she was going to react within her wife sphere to her husband's desire to get into drag racing.

Wendy had been working on staying on track for some time. She knew that the marriage was partially built around what she brought to it through her participation in it. She could bring barriers to individuality and indulge insecurities or she could bring courage and support to the marriage. She decided the kind of wife she wanted to be was one who supported individual growth, a wife who respected and encouraged her husband's individuality and his partnership with her. She did not want to be the kind of married woman who tried to prevent Bob from pursuing his interests in life, no more than she would want him to be husband who naysayed her own interests. She decided to support him!

When Bob told her about his interest and conveyed his enthusiasm, she said, "Oh, Bob, so far, racing really scares me but I can tell you want to do it. How can I help? Let's go slowly and talk about it so I can learn how to join you on this. I like what you said about families enjoying drag racing together." Wendy did a great job of bringing to her marriage the principle that successful marriages support healthy individual activities.

Compare her response to Donna's, when her husband James wanted to include an old girlfriend in plans to go to a funeral. Donna and James had been married for five years, but long before they were married,

SUPPORTING INDIVIDUAL DIFFERENCES

James had been involved with Sue. At that time, James and Sue both worked in real estate, saw each other in professional settings and had a previous boss named Dave, whom they both greatly admired. After a long struggle with cancer, Dave had died. Knowing that Sue cared for Dave, James asked her if she wanted to go to Dave's funeral with him and Donna. When he told Donna of this, she hit the roof: "How could you invite an old girlfriend to go to a funeral with us? How dare you include her on the same level with me? You are incredibly insensitive to my feelings." Donna was so angry she refused to go to Dave's funeral!

Clearly, Donna is dumping her insecurities into her marriage. By making a stink about Sue accompanying them, she is being a married woman who creates a barrier to James' good-natured and mature desire to include Sue in the mourning of Dave's death. James isn't asking Sue for a date, he isn't proposing an intimate relationship with her, he is simply acknowledging a common bond around their friendship with Dave and offering to jointly honor this bond by asking her to attend Dave's funeral together with him and Donna. After five years of marriage Donna's concern about old girlfriends, especially in the context of an old friend's funeral, is an unworkable marital attitude for her. Wendy's way of being a married woman works better than Donna's. Wendy supports appropriate individuality; Donna opposes it.

Successful marriages not only allow for individuality, they foster individual growth. These marriages do not erect barriers to individual activities and growth, but rather welcome them as a healthy part of life and marriage. Whether your husband wants to begin racing cars or boats, or explore a change in careers, or invite an old girlfriend and colleague to a funeral, be a married woman who helps him do it, not a wife who protests or tries to prevent his wish from happening. Marriage includes, "I-ness" and "we-ness," individuality and togetherness. A balance of each needs to be maintained. This balance allows for two individuals to be married. Stay on track and support both individuality and partnership in your marriage.

MARRIAGE MAKEOVER

STEP EIGHTEEN

Being a Wife and a Mother

*How to maintain being a
wife when you have children.*

IF YOU HAVE CHILDREN, you have two roles in the family: You are a wife and a mother. Because the two roles often interact with one another, it is helpful to know the difference between your role as a wife and your role as a mother.

We all know that if your child is in danger, or ill, you will put aside other roles and take care of your child. If your child needs you, then your primary responsibility at the moment is to him or her. However, the central and long-term role in your family as a married woman is wife. It is the husband and wife who form the core of the family. The marriage you both create is the center post of the family.

The marriage is the place in the family where differences about parenting are best resolved. If you have a disagreement about the kids, it is best resolved as wife and husband. Let's say, you (the mother) and your husband, (the father) disagree about setting a bedtime for the kids. He thinks the kids should have staggered bedtimes according to age. Peter, who is two years older than Kendra, should be able to stay up a half hour later. You think they should both go to bed at the same time.

Where in the family structure is it best to put this disagreement? If you put it in the mother and father place, you may never solve it. Your bedtime ideas are good and so are his. Neither position is unreasonable. You could probably find parenting advice to back up either side of the debate. One parent will have to give in to the other, creating a winner and a loser. However, if you put the disagreement in the marriage, it is resolvable. You have the marital tools to reach resolution. How? Stay on track! If you stay on track and remain true to your action values, you will be able to talk about it, listen, take time out if it gets heated, and apply the caring and consideration in your action values to the resolution of the differences between you. Staying on track as a wife allows you to bring all the effectiveness and good will of your action values to the resolution of parenting differences. When the parents of Peter and Kendra placed the disagreement into the domain of their marriage, they decided to try each bedtime approach for two weeks, then to have a family meeting and evaluate the results. Based on the results they—wife and husband— would decide what to do as mother and father. Moving the disagreement from the parental roles to the marital roles, kept them from creating an impasse.

Another way of conceptualizing the difference between being a wife and a mother, is to hug your husband with the children present. You will notice that if the kids are less than about eight years old, they will typically want in on the hugging. When hugging the kids, you are mom and dad. When hugging only each other, you are wife and husband. The kids want to make you into mom and dad hugging by including themselves. Tell them, "right now, I'm hugging my husband. In a second you can get in on it." Then bring the kids in and tell them, "Now this is a family hug." Not only are you teaching the kids that the family structure includes not only a mother and father, but a wife and husband, as well. You are reminding yourself, too. In many families adult family roles acquire an imbalance with the woman being mother almost all the time and the father being father almost all the time. The marriage gets lost in the parenting. When the kids begin their search for independence in their early teens, these marriages are weak and are sometimes unable to achieve transition as the ratio between spouse and parent inevitably changes In these families, there is often not much marriage left to build a future upon. In marriages where wife and husband roles are swallowed up by mom and dad roles, problems typically show up near the time of the children's transition into independence: the kids test the limits in dangerous way, affairs begin, the partners drift apart or divorce. It is best to keep a healthy balance and respect toward being a wife and a mom, right from the start. Not only will you have a healthier marriage but a healthier family, too.

MARRIAGE MAKEOVER
STEP NINETEEN

How to Maintain Romance

Romance is both inspiration and skill.

ROMANCE IS ACTING IN INTIMATE and loving ways toward your husband. Most married women want to be romantic. Romance is fun, and both wife and husband enjoy its presence. A lot of married women are good at romance. They know how to include it in their marriage on a regular basis. Most married women can get better at being romantic—there is always room for improvement. I recommend that all wives put "romantic" on their action value list. This will help you focus on romance and build it into your daily marital life. Romance is one of those activities in life where more comes back to you than you give. It feels better whether you are giving or receiving. Romance is exponential—a little becomes a lot. Married women who are good at romance have more fun in their marriage. Here are some ideas for getting better at romance.

Romance is part inspiration and part skill. The inspiration comes from feelings of love and the skill part comes from knowledge—knowing how to be romantic, what to do and how to do it.

For romance to have meaning and feel authentic, it must originate from feelings of love. Love makes romance real and not just a technique. When you are romantic, you are saying, "You are my love, my lover, my sweetheart."

HOW TO MAINTAIN ROMANCE

Romance is the heart speaking the love you feel for your husband.

Romance is also a skill. It is made up of actions that you can get good at through knowledge and practice.

To get good at romance, first see it as an expression of the love you feel for your husband. It is a way of letting him know that you love him through intimate actions and words. The love connection makes your romantic actions authentic and real. Without it, acts of intimacy will seem sterile and barren. Broaden your view of romance. Don't confuse romance with sex. Romance isn't sex but sex can be romantic. Learn that intimacy, sex, and general playfulness all play a part in romance.

Rachel shows her love for her husband, Nick, when she walks by his seated place in the kitchen and gently squeezes his shoulder. She also shows her love when she calls after a doctor appointment to ask Nick how he is. She also shows her love by setting up a sexy encounter in the bedroom with oils and candles.

Make romance a consistent part of being a wife. Organize your romance so that it occurs all year long, and not just on special occasions such as Valentine's Day. Do this by marking dates to be romantic on your private calendar. Go through the calendar for each month and arbitrarily select a day on which to be romantic. Write your husband's initials on the selected day. Make sure the chosen day is a non-special occasion so that it comes as a surprise. Do not choose a birthday, anniversary, or holiday for your surprise romantic day. Chances are the special days will be celebrated anyway. Make your surprise romantic day an extra day of romance. On the chosen day of each month, do something that shows your love for your husband. Here are some romantic ideas.

On your chosen day in January, send your husband flowers at his work place with a simple note, "I love you."

In February celebrate Valentines Day, but also on another day of the month, send him a card to your home address expressing how much you love him, how much he means to you.

One day in March, put a post-it note on the shower wall opposite the faucet where it won't get washed away. On the note, write his name and "you're my guy. You sure look good. Love, (name).

In April, call him at work (if he has a job where this is not a problem) and engage in small talk. When he asks what you want, tell him that you were just thinking about him and wanted to tell him that.

In May, get a nice little bouquet of flowers and put it on his dresser. Just flowers, no note. Contrary to some popular notions, most men like to get flowers.

In June, put a cassette or CD in his car stereo. Set it to play a love song. Put a post-it note on the dash, saying, "Hit the play button for an important message."

In July, hide a romantic card in his lunch box, tool case, brief case—whatever he carries to work—so that he will unexpectedly find it sometime during the day.

In August, leave a love note in the pocket of a jacket he wears a lot, so that when he reaches into his pocket he will find it.

This gives you the idea of how to make romance a regular part of everyday life. There are dozens of books available with hundreds of suggestions for being more fun, more intriguing, and sexier. As you think of more ideas, put them on your calendar to complete the year. Don't forget obvious romantic gestures such as walks in the moonlight, candles at dinner, low lighting, romantic music, and being naked together.

There is probably no aspect of being a married woman where more comes back to you than what you have given. It feels good to be romantic. It is compounded interest in your marital bank account and then some. A little bit can become a lot. All wives, for their own growth and fulfillment, as well as for the success of their marriage, should get good at maintaining romance.

PART SIX: MARITAL PROBLEMS OR MENTAL PROBLEMS?

MARRIAGE MAKEOVER

STEP TWENTY

Resolving: Is it We or Is it Me?

How to determine if you are suffering from an emotional disorder or a marital problem.

JUDY AND HER HUSBAND, DANNY, came to see me for marital therapy. Judy looked a wreck. She was having trouble sleeping and was tired all the time. She was emotionally frazzled, overreacting to the slightest nuance of distance or criticism from Danny. She admitted to being "bitchy" most of the time. However, she had her good days, too. These were her periods of calm when she was more resilient, less reactive. Her husband read about manic-depression (bipolar illness) in the local newspaper and wondered if this was causing Judy's fluctuations in mood and energy. When he brought it up, Judy thought he was calling her crazy and avoiding his own problems. Inwardly, however, she wondered if she did have a mental problem. "I can't be this upset, this unhappy, this distraught, unless there is something wrong with me," she often thought to herself.

Is Judy "crazy" or is she in a marriage in which she or Danny, or both, are seriously off track? Is she suffering from a psychiatric disorder, or just reacting emotionally and mentally to the disorder of the marriage? I have seen so many wives and husbands come into my office looking as though they have a psychiatric disorder, that I have come to the conclusion that anybody can look critically disturbed in the midst of a seriously troubled marriage. While some women (and men) who are in troubled marriages do suffer from a mental disorder, most do not.

But they wonder, "do I have these moods swings because I feel up one minute and down the next in my marriage, or because I have a bi-polar illness (manic-depressive disorder)? Do I have trouble sleeping, experience almost no appetite at all, feel lethargic, cry easily, and feel discouraged because I am so unhappily married, or because I am clinically depressed? Am I suspicious of my husband's activities because he withholds information and I don't know where he spends his time, or because I have paranoid tendencies? Am I in an emotional rage most of the time because my marriage is a wreck, or because I have an anger problem? Do I drink too much because I am trying to numb myself to the unhappiness of my marriage, or because I have a chemical dependency problem?" A wife who is withdrawn in her marriage can seem depressed. A wife who is nervous and unable to sleep well, can appear to be suffering from an anxiety disorder. A wife who drinks too much, can look chemically dependent. No matter how she may describe herself when she arrives in the therapist's office, a wife in a troubled marriage can appear to be seriously and clinically disturbed when she is not. A chronically unsuccessful marriage can make you look and feel "crazy" when you are, in reality, affected by the marital situation, rather than an internal state of chemical or cognitive disturbance.

The best way I know to distinguish whether you are experiencing a troubled marriage and therefore, look depressed, anxious, paranoid, chemically dependent, etc., or whether you are actually suffering from a clinical disorder, is to do your absolute utmost to get on track and see how well you do. If you are able to get on track, chances are you are a healthy and normal adult married woman. Being on track requires that you become individuated, value centered, and able to guide yourself from your values, instead of your urges to react. This is no small feat and if you are able to do it, you are displaying resiliency and emotional health. However, if you sincerely try to get on track and despite your best efforts, you just cannot do it, then you may be carrying the additional burden of a clinical disorder into your marital efforts. You may have a depressive, anxiety, personality, or chemical dependency disorder that requires treatment beyond marital attempts to get on track.

Here are two examples of clinical disorders that required resolution so a married woman could get on track in her marriage. The first example is a woman suffering from a moderate obsessive-compulsive personality disorder (OCPD), and how she resolved this problem. The second example is a married woman experiencing posttraumatic stress disorder (PTSD), caused from being sexually abused as a child.

OBSESSIVE COMPULSIVE PERSONALITY DISORDER

If you are chronically bothered by "everything needing to get done" and you constantly think your husband and other family members are not doing their share, then you may be suffering from obsessive-compulsive personality disorder (OCPD). Characterized by a preoccupation with orderliness, OCPD is a desire for perfectionism, a focus on tasks at the exclusion of leisure activities, a reluctance to allocate tasks, and inflexibility and rigidity.

A wife suffering from OCPD usually complains bitterly about being overwhelmed by tasks and can't understand why her husband doesn't see what needs to be done and pitch in. Usually this is not because a husband isn't bothered by tasks needing attention, it is because the wife is bothered instantly by everything that needs to be done, and she believes that only she is capable of doing it right. "Everything needs to be done now and I need to do it or it won't get done," is the silent and insidious mantra that drives these wives' actions. Such a compulsively driven married woman is chronically frustrated and unhappy. She generally complains—openly or silently—on a continual basis. Because she has a compulsive need to keep everything near perfect, she drives herself and her husband crazy.

NANCY'S STORY

Nancy had been married for nearly 25 years. She was highly successful at work where she was considered absolutely reliable and dependable. "If you want something done, give it to Nancy and you know it will get done and on time, always," was Nancy's reputation at work. While this approach had served her well at work, it led to a miserable existence at home. She had chronic stomachaches and had gone to bed with a headache most nights for a long time. Life at home was a constant irritant. She complained but nobody seemed to listen. She couldn't seem to help herself, everything needed to be done, she seemed to be the only one willing to do it, and no one would help her.

If you were to talk to Nancy's husband, Mel, he would tell you he is more than willing to help with household tasks, but Nancy does it first. Or, if he does it she goes behind him and does it again. For example, if he cleans the bathroom, she wipes everything down after him. If he says he'll do the shopping, she does it on her way home from work. If their kids agree to clean their rooms on Sunday, Nancy is in there picking, sorting and hanging up clothes on Saturday. Mel and the kids know she is unhappy and they tell her to relax, let them do it, it will get done, but she goes ahead and does it anyway. She can't help herself. She works and works, and goes to bed exhausted every night.

In marital therapy, Nancy did her best to get on track. Her list of action values was excellent and doable. Try as she might, she could not get over crushing feelings of resentment when her family didn't help as she wanted. She felt angry with her husband every minute of every day because he didn't anticipate what needed to be done around the house, and because she ended up doing everything. However, on the occasions when he and the kids pitched in to do their part, she felt guilty and restless. It was a no-win situation. The unremitting feelings of anger overwhelmed her attempts to get on track. When she would try to be affectionate, supportive or positive as a wife, her feelings of anger would surface and she would return to complaining and criticizing her husband. When it became apparent that Nancy was carrying the additional burden of OCPD into her efforts to get on track and OCPD tendencies were a major obstacle that needed individual attention, marital therapy was reorganized to include a combination of couple and individual sessions to address both her desire to get on track and to resolve her OCPD.

Many effective psychotherapy techniques are available for figuring out how to rid yourself of obsessive-compulsive behaviors. I typically recommend a cognitive-behavioral therapy approach because compulsions seem to me to be driven by how a person thinks. Cognitive-behavioral means thoughts-actions. In cognitive-behavioral therapy a person sorts out the thoughts that generate and support his or her behaviors so that a new reality can offer greater flexibility, adaptation and contentment. Nancy agreed to work with me on a cognitive-behavioral approach to her OCPD tendencies. Therapy was arranged with a schedule of three individual sessions and one marital session so that the progress she made personally could be blended into marital efforts to get on track. The joint sessions also helped Mel get on track and to appreciate and understand Nancy's progress.

Nancy worked hard at resolving her obsessive-compulsive thoughts and behavior. She learned how to dispel physiological tension through progressive relaxation exercises, how to institute worry behavior prevention strategies, how to be a better problem solver, how to manage time better, and how to challenge and restructure her obsessive-compulsive thoughts. Soon she was able to "hear" herself as she had thoughts that drove her to be bothered and compelled her toward perfectionism. She developed the ability to challenge and change these thoughts into more realistic inner statements guiding her to act in moderate ways towards tasks. As she accomplished this, her feelings of anger and resentment subsided and she felt more at ease with herself and her surroundings. As she resolved her obsessive-compulsive tendencies, Nancy was able to work effectively on getting on track in her marriage. She no longer felt compelled to do everything, her stomach trouble and headaches stopped and she was able to work normally on her attempts to get on track in her marriage. Nancy discovered that once obsessive-compulsive problems are resolved, staying on track becomes a much easier endeavor, and a more equal allocation of household tasks a reachable goal. Eventually, Nancy and Mel got on track in their marriage, and both shared in doing household tasks as part of being married successfully. Occasionally Nancy would feel some of her old urges to rush into taking care of household chores, but as she did, she would look into her mind, calm herself down, examine her thoughts, change or challenge them as needed, and resolve her feelings of compulsion. Over time, she got pretty good at being on track, resolved her OCPD and felt quite proud of what she had accomplished.

POST-TRAUMATIC STRESS DISORDER

Here is the heart-wrenching story of a young woman who tried to get on track but was unable to do so until she resolved her Post-Traumatic Stress Disorder (PTSD). Although serious and debilitating, PTSD can be overcome. Tricia challenged her PTSD and got on track in her marriage.

RESOLVING: IS IT WE OR IS IT ME?

TRICIA'S STORY

Tricia was 28 years old and had worked herself up to mid-level accountant, when she met Ron, a 36 years old and third generation Japanese American. He came to work for the firm as an accountant specializing in business audits. He was shy, much like Tricia, yet friendly and very polite. When a coworker friend of Tricia's found out that Ron was single, she began to plan their meeting. She persuaded Tricia to go out with Ron, if he asked her. Tricia had noticed Ron, and liked his sincerity and quiet politeness. Soon, Ron was told that Tricia was single, and that if he asked her out, she would say yes. Ron had very little experience dating, but got up his nerve and asked Tricia out. Their first date was an afternoon at the zoo.

Tricia liked Ron from the very first date and Ron felt the same. His reserve easily endeared her to him. They began to enjoy quiet times together—walks in the park, movies, dinners out—and grew to spending Sundays together reading and fixing light meals. Neither was forward about intimacy, indulging in some hugging and kissing but nothing more. After six months of dating, Tricia met Ron's family. She liked their gracious manners, and especially their circumspect questions about her family. They were not pushy and especially not nosy. They were obviously pleased Ron had met someone he liked.

Soon after this meeting, Ron asked Tricia to marry him and she accepted. One Sunday, they drove to Tricia's parents so Ron could meet them. Tricia warned Ron not to expect much because she was not close to her family, the way Ron was close to his. Ron accepted this, and the meeting went well enough for both Ron and Tricia to feel they had passed their "family" hurdles. As for sexual intimacy, both Ron and Tricia decided to wait until after marriage to engage in intercourse. Ron was comfortable with this because he was shy and inexperienced about sex, and Tricia felt relieved because of her sexual uncertainties and fears.

She felt, however, that her love for Ron would in time overcome feelings of sexual confusion and insecurity.

Ron had not been raised in a particularly religious family and Tricia wanted nothing to do with her parents' religion, so wedding plans turned toward a civil ceremony. Tricia was relieved at this because she couldn't imagine walking down the aisle with her father and him giving her away.

With a few friends from the office and the presence of both sets of parents, Tricia and Ron were married by a judge in a small reception hall at a local hotel. A reception followed and Tricia and Ron left for a weekend honeymoon at a lakeside lodge a few hours drive from home. They had already arranged to live in Ron's apartment when they returned.

While sex was awkward for both, it was without trauma. Tricia felt she could trust Ron, and this helped her give herself to him. Tricia could tell Ron was sexually inexperienced, and this helped her feel relaxed about closeness. The honeymoon weekend went well. Tricia and Ron returned home pleased with their marriage, and looking forward to a good life together. Tricia felt her past life was over and she had a new start. She deeply loved Ron and she felt sure her love would see her through whatever lay ahead.

About four months into the marriage, Tricia began having troublesome dreams. She would wake up in the night sweaty and scared. Ron slept soundly so she was able to hide her awakenings from him. The bad dreams would come and go, and soon Tricia figured out the dreams occurred only on nights when they had sex. This worried her—was her past coming back to haunt her—so she doubled her efforts to love Ron. It didn't help—the sex-and-bad-dreams association continued. Soon, Tricia was using excuses to avoid sex with Ron. At first he was understanding, then he began to withdraw himself. As he withdrew, Tricia felt abandoned and scared. She became more and more isolated, refusing to go out except to work or for necessities. Evenings became occasions of mostly silence until it was time for bed. Most nights, Tricia lay awake fearful that Ron would want sex. Troublesome dreams persisted. At work she had difficulty concentrating. She became quiet and withdrawn. Soon, she had periods when she hid in the bathroom and cried. Ron was no help. He felt confused and bewildered. If he tried to be close to Tricia, she pulled away. He asked her what was troubling her but she just clammed up. He began to bring work home and took to sitting for hours in front of the computer. Marriage was not going well for either of them and Tricia felt miserable—like it was all her fault. If only she could tell Ron what was troubling her, but she couldn't get herself to do this. Opening up was too frightening.

One night Ron asked Tricia if she would go to marriage counseling with him. He had confided in a college friend that he and Tricia were estranged from one another in their marriage, and the friend suggested counseling. Tricia agreed. She didn't want to fail in her marriage, and she didn't want to lose Ron. Ron and Tricia made an appointment to see me.

When I first saw Tricia and Ron in my office, they presented themselves as a couple that was distant and uncommunicative. Their marriage had lost its vitality. Both were seriously off track and acting out hurt feelings rather than loving ones. They agreed to come in and work on improving their marriage.

Marital therapy went through the course outlined so far in this book, covering commitment and identifying action values. Eventually, both began working at getting on track. Tricia chose to work specifically on her action values of sharing, being attentive and being a good listener. These action values allowed Tricia to safely get started on her work with being on track. Ron chose to become more patient, upbeat, and open. These too, were good starter action values for Ron. Progress was steady, until each had focused on all his and her action values except ones dealing with intimacy, affection and sex. After they had gone home to attempt getting on track in these delicate areas of their marriage, they returned to my office silent and withdrawn. It was like they had regressed to the same marriage I had seen on their first visit. I asked if I could see each of them in an individual session. Both agreed.

In my session with Ron, he told me of his sexual inexperience and insecurities, but described no history of trauma in his development as a child, adolescent or young adult. He had always been an introvert and his sexual insecurities were consistent with his history of shyness. He expressed a desire to be affectionate, intimate and sexual with Tricia. He wondered if he had done something to hurt her and make her feel afraid of him. Neither of us was able to identify anything that appeared purposely hurtful or threatening. Ron had become withdrawn as a husband, but not inconsiderate.

Tricia seemed quite frightened at our individual session. She sat with her arms folded around her and her eyes downcast. She was able to talk in general terms about her past and shared with me a history of being a shy, capable and quiet child, adolescent and young adult. However, when I asked her to describe the relationship she had with her father, she fell silent. As she sat there, I could see her struggle to speak. Finally, she said in a whisper, "My father sexually abused me." Not surprisingly, this bit of history explained a lot.

Tricia's father began sexually abusing her when she was a toddler and by the time she was eight years old, he was forcing her to have sexual intercourse. From the outside, the family looked normal. Her parents were religiously conservative and took Tricia and her younger brother to church every Sunday. The family prayed at every meal and Tricia was made to say her prayers before bedtime. Outside of the public eye the family was in disarray. After bedtime prayers and after the other family members were asleep, Tricia's father would often sneak into her bedroom and force her to have sex with him. Up until she was eight or nine he told her what a good girl she was, that he loved her, and that she was special. When she got to be nearly ten, he threatened to punish her or leave her late in the night in some dark alley downtown, if she told anyone what he did to her. Tricia was terrified of him. She avoided him whenever she could. Her mother thought she was a strange child, exceedingly polite and deferent to others, but moody and distant at home. She often asked Tricia if something was the matter. One day when Tricia was eleven, she told her mother that her father forced intercourse on her when he came into her room late at night. Tricia's mother was shocked. She said she would talk to Tricia's father. A few days went by, and finally, Tricia's mother confronted Tricia for lying. Tricia was put on restriction, with no television and an early bedtime. A few nights later, when her father came into her room and forced himself upon her, he told Tricia that nobody would believe her, that she was a bad girl for telling, that he was the one who bought her clothes and provided a roof over her head, that she owed him his time with her, and that she had better not say anything to anyone again, or she would suffer even greater punishment. Tricia felt completely alone, frightened, humiliated and powerless.

This pattern of sexual abuse continued until Tricia turned sixteen, when she ran away from home to live with her boyfriend and his family. Tricia was a polite and bashful teenager, who clung to her boyfriend. She would do anything for him, if only he would keep her as his girlfriend. She let him have sex with her whenever he wanted. Sex was almost a routine for her, with little feeling of closeness or intimacy. She seemed to "check out" in her mind during sex. Tricia privately carried the burden of the sexual abuse she had suffered from her father. She never told her boyfriend, his parents, a teacher, or a counselor about her father's abuse of her. She felt ashamed. However, she was a bright and exemplary student at school. Teachers and school officials thought well of her but for the most part tended not to give her particular notice. Tricia got by as best she could with her secret intact.

Tricia finished high school. Oddly enough, her boyfriend did break up with her when he left home for college a year before Tricia finished high school. At first, Tricia was in a panic that she would have to go back to her parents' house. She pleaded with her boyfriend's parents to let her continue to live with them. Liking Tricia they relented and allowed her to continue living with them until her graduation. They even helped her financially until she graduated, got a night job stocking shelves at a large department store and saved enough money to get an apartment with one of the girls she met at work. Tricia enrolled in afternoon classes at the local community college and began life as a young adult woman on her own. While she was glad to be away from her family, she felt alienated and scared, especially about relationships. She went to work, school and home, and pretty much stayed to herself.

Tricia avoided men as best she could. Although pretty, she dressed in loose clothes, used little make-up and avoided social situations. She did not want to draw the attention of men. She had little in common with the social life of girls her age, felt tainted by her father's sexual abuse of her, and wondered if she wasn't seriously troubled as an individual.

Life went on for Tricia and finally she finished community college. She pulled up stakes, moving two hundred miles from home where she enrolled in a four-year college as an accounting major. She got a room in the home of an elderly woman and for help in caring for her, paid no rent. Tricia was able to transfer her job to a companion department store near school. Work and school where safe places were she felt okay. She knew what was expected of her and if she did her work, completed her studies, and stayed to herself; nobody bothered her.

RESOLVING: IS IT WE OR IS IT ME?

After finishing college, Tricia got a job as an assistant accountant. She found a nice apartment, decorated it, acquired a cat and settled in. Her quiet and controlled life went smoothly. She tried not to think about her childhood sexual abuse. She visited her family for holidays and joined in the game of denial, pretending nothing untoward had happened between her and her father. She treated him with distance and politeness, and he was quiet and self-righteous toward her. The cover-up of secrets was part of the dysfunctional instability in the family and Tricia was automatically a part of it. In this family, denial was business as usual. However, she never stayed overnight, preferring to drive the four hours back and forth in one day. An overnight stay would have been too scary.

Upon hearing this I suspected that Tricia was suffering from the symptoms of a chronic post-traumatic stress disorder (PTSD). This was confirmed when she shared information with me about disturbed dreams, feelings of unreality, flashbacks, attempts to avoid thoughts about her father, diminished interest in activities, poor concentration, feelings of detachment from Ron and spells of crying. I expressed to Tricia my impression that she was suffering from PTSD. She had heard about it. I asked if she would like to work on resolving it and she said she would. We then talked over how to best approach resolution of PTSD.

I explained my reasons for thinking that resolution of PTSD would help, but probably not be enough in its own right, to address the goal of having a successful marriage with Ron. I told her I thought we should continue to include Ron every third session so that his and her work with getting on track could continue. She agreed. I then recommended that I have a session with both of them and she could tell Ron that she had been sexually abused. He would then know what was going on and I could help him shape a "husband" response towards her work of resolving her PTSD. She felt very frightened by this idea, but when I explained that central features of sexual abuse are secrets and deception, and that a commitment on her part to stop keeping secrets would be essential to resolving the effects of having been abused, she understood and agreed that telling Ron would be a good start. Also, I had gotten to know Ron, and I felt fairly certain he would have a considerate and understanding response to learning about Tricia's experience of being abused.

In a joint session with Ron, she told him about having been sexually abused by her father, but without going into great detail. Predictably, Ron was shocked by what he heard, but sympathetic to her feelings. While it was difficult for Tricia to tell Ron, she was relieved to get it out in the open, and heartened by Ron's non-judgmental response. Tricia agreed to come in every week for as long as it would take to resolve the effects of the sexual abuse, and Ron agreed to joint sessions every third visit, so that efforts to work on a successful marriage could continue.

This arrangement continued for 18 months. Tricia worked exceedingly hard on overcoming the effects of the sexual abuse she had suffered in her childhood. Eventually, she no longer experienced disturbing dreams and flashbacks, she was able to recall many of the details of her experiences without extreme and debilitating emotionality, her crying stopped, and her concentration and overall mood improved. Through carefully constructed letters to her father, she clearly placed the responsibility of the abuse on him. He finally admitted his culpability to her. Tricia informed her mother and brother of the abuse, and declared her unwillingness any longer to be the repository of kept secrets in the family. What her family needed to do to adjust to the impact of long held and tragic secrets coming into the open, was left up to them. Tricia accepted responsibility only for deciding what she wanted to be like as an adult daughter in the family.

In regular joint sessions with Ron, she shared her struggles and progress with him, learning to be open in her marriage, and to be trusting of a man with whom she was close and emotionally vulnerable. Ron remained considerate and supportive throughout. He was challenged in therapy to stay on track being the husband he wanted to be, as Tricia progressed through her emotional work. In every joint session, ratings were done of his action values, as well as Tricia's, so that the focus was maintained on their goal to have a successful marriage. When therapy ended, Tricia still experienced some discomfort while engaging in affection, intimacy and sex with Ron. However, she was able to talk about it, recognize its origins, and work on it by concentrating on being on track affectionately and sexually. Her efforts to resolve her PTSD, blended well with her efforts to be on track with her action values as a wife. As she progressively resolved her feelings, she got better at being affectionate, intimate, sexual and romantic, the action values for being the married woman she wanted to be. In the end she understood that it could take years for the residual effects of PTSD to have no affect on her, but that if she continued her efforts to be on track, the effects would eventually resolve themselves.

FIRST—GET ON TRACK

Tricia and Nancy's stories could have been about any married woman trying to get on track but being unable to do so because of established disorders: adult attention-deficit disorder, addiction disorder, anxiety disorder, psychotic disorder, mood disorder, somatoform disorder (an unexplainable medical condition believed to be caused by a psychological condition), factitious disorder (physical or psychological symptoms that are intentionally produced or feigned in order to assume the sick role), sexual and gender identity disorder, impulse disorder, personality disorder, or medical condition such as a hormone imbalance. All of these conditions require specific and effective treatment in their own right, and all of them can affect attempts to get on track. The caveat here is that if you have followed the precepts of this book, doing the best you can to get on track, and despite your best efforts you are unable to do so, then seek help from someone highly trained not only in marital therapy, but across the board in psychology or psychiatry. Find out if some condition exists that prevents you from having the emotional resiliency to get on track. If a disorder is blocking your way get treatment for it while continuing to work at being on track in your marriage.

In nearly a quarter century of providing psychological services, I have come to the conclusion that any and all disorders have a remarkable chance of getting resolved through effective treatment. I have also found that in the vast majority of cases, a married woman in a seriously troubled marriage is not, for instance, suffering from clinical depression, an anxiety disorder, or PTSD, but can appear so in the stormy chaos of a distressed marriage. Before you come to any conclusion about yourself and whether you are suffering from a clinical disorder, first, try to get on track.

PART SEVEN: REACHING FULFILLMENT

MARRIAGE MAKEOVER
STEP TWENTY ONE

Being Your Best Self

Did Cheryl become fulfilled?

I HOPE THAT READING THIS BOOK has helped you figure out how to be married successfully. Now, where do you go from here? What more can you get from your journey as a married woman? My wish for you is that you get on track, and get better at consistently being on track, so that you can eventually realize your higher self as a wife. Attaining your higher self requires that you begin thinking about all that you can become as a married woman.

The Greek philosopher, Aristotle, has a term for this process-result in life that he calls "entelechy." It means that everything that exists has a form, and inherent in its form, is what it can become. For instance, being on track as a married woman for long periods of life, is like a minister praying for years and over time experiencing an ever-deepening relationship between herself and her God. It is like a musician playing a musical instrument, and finding an ever-deepening sense of expression as she gets increasingly more adept at expressing herself musically. It is like a poet writing poetry for years, going back to her first compositions, and realizing what a compelling path she followed to the place represented by her present poetry. You are a married woman, and inherent in your wife sphere—your action values for being a wife—is what you can become as a married woman. Realizing your higher self as a married woman is reaching toward the best of what you can be, stopping for a moment on the way and reflecting how good you feel about yourself as who you are, and then going on with the business of life of being a married woman who is on track.

How can you reach the best of what you can be as a married woman? Is there a great secret here, or a mystery that must be unraveled? No, all it requires is to be clear of mind and heart, accept responsibility for yourself, work hard at being on track, persist, and stay with it as the years unfold. In other words, be clear that you are an adult woman choosing to be a wife, that you accept what exists within your domain as married woman and what is separate from it, and that you keep in mind your action values and try to remain true to them through all aspects of marriage. That you trust your experience as a married woman will grow over the years as you do this. You are "in process" and with time will become more of who you are as a married woman than you are presently. You don't have to be good at being on track from the start, in order to begin the road toward your higher self. You just have to decide to be married, work hard at getting on track, stick with it, get good at it, and your self-actualization as a married woman will naturally evolve and emerge over time. The more you "do" your action values—express the best of your human qualities as a married woman—the greater will be your experience of fulfillment.

Another way of conceptualizing this process is to look at your action values for being on track, how they relate to positive human qualities, and how you might rate them over time. Chances are, your action values represent positive human qualities in general, applied to be being a married woman in particular. If we look back at Cheryl's list we see action values such as being loving, positive, trusting, expressive, a good listener, open minded, intimate, respectful, and nice. Now, imagine what will happen if Cheryl gets on track with these action values, works hard to stay on track, persists across all marital situations, and sticks with it for years and years? She will get better and better and more genuine and spontaneous, at being loving, being positive, trusting, being expressive, listening, being intimate, and respecting. By working on action values over the years that extend her better self, Cheryl will have become more of who she can be as the married woman she wants to be. Now, add to Cheryl's staying on track in her marriage:

- the reasonable and rational choice to be a married woman,
- the promise to do whatever she can to solve problems,
- the pledge of non-iffy loving,
- the assurance she will remain faithful,

and what Cheryl has is the potential for self-actualization and fulfillment as a married woman. Within this self-actualization, she can experience fulfillment, in other words, realize fully her potential as a married woman. This is the way our potential is fully realized for all of us in our marriages, not just Cheryl. Put as simply as possible, being committed, and staying on track with your action values for years and years, can result in fulfillment and realization of your higher self as a married woman.

The realization of your higher self does not occur everyday. As you continue to stay on track moments of reflection will occur, times when you focus on yourself, how good you feel, and how well you are doing. At these times of self-appraisal, you will know whether or not you are doing well at being on track. If you are, then warm feelings of contentment and satisfaction will sweep through you. You will be proud of yourself for what you have accomplished. Being a married woman will feel fulfilling and satisfying. This moment of satisfying reflection of your potential will pass and you will go on to the everyday job of being married until something causes you to reflect again. This cycle—doing it, feeling it, appraising it, and back to doing it—will seesaw throughout your marital life. While you will be working on your potential all along the way, you will only be aware of it during times of reflection. The rest of the time you will be busy doing it.

Self-actualization is not, however, self-absorption. Truly self-actualized woman are fully engaged in marital life, and only on occasion find themselves assessing their state of being as a married woman. But occasionally, a question from a child, a story from a book, a song, a conversation with your husband about past events in your lives, will trigger self-reflection and at these moments of self-appraisal, the pride and fulfillment as a married woman can be appreciated and your higher self acknowledged.

Staying on track and reaching a self-actualized state as a married woman also prepares you for moments of genuine connection with your husband. By being on track, you are in a ready state for a close bonding with your husband. In this state of self-actualized readiness, you bring to the marital inbetween an open regard and acceptance of your husband as the person he is. You present your authentic married self and this self evokes no judgment of him as a husband. In a small way, it is like expressing your opinion with absolutely no sense that there is anything wrong with him for having a different view. His opinions are honored as coming from a separate person who is in conjunction with "I," without judgment. In your self-actualized state, you are so on track that you are authentically open in your presentation of who you are and this allows him, if he can, to connect to you fully as a person. You connect with him in your fullness as a person, and this enables him to connect to you in his fullness as a person. When this kind of human/marital connecting occurs, you will feel confirmed as the unique human being/ married woman that you are. I truly believe that it is the human-connecting-to-human realm of life where we find out who we authentically have become, and that marriage is such a fully engaged adult relationship that it constitutes the place where such humanness is most likely to occur in our lives. And, it is your higher self as a married woman that makes this fully inter-human, marital connecting possible. What you can become as a married woman is as boundless as who you can become as a person, and marriage is a place where the reaching of your human confirmation can occur.

The question naturally arises, "What does my husband have to do with my self-actualization as a wife, and whether I have authentic moments of humanness in my relationship with him?" The answer is, quite a lot but not everything. Remember earlier in this book, where I discussed the job of being on track as the married woman you want to be, and I said that your husband can make it hard or easy but, ultimately, he will never be in charge of what you are like as a wife. This is as true with your higher self and the experience of your full humanness in relationship to him, as it is with any level of being a married woman. Just keep in mind, that if, in your turn toward your husband, you are on track and unconditionally accepting of his humanness, you bring to the meeting between you and him the ingredients of self-actualization and human togetherness. Bringing the ingredients is all you can do. Your husband can make it hard or easy for you be your higher self, but he will never be in charge of whether you are or not. As long as you remain on track as best you can, you are doing all you can possibly do so that your higher self occurs and genuine humanness unfolds between you and him.

Whether you are trying to survive a troubled marriage, search for fulfillment, seek self-actualization, or evoke authentic togetherness, staying on track marks the place to start and the course to follow.

HOW CHERYL REALIZED HER HIGHER SELF

The process toward self-actualization and interpersonal humanness begins exactly where Cheryl began—with introducing rational ideas about commitment, with identifying action values, with learning how to manage staying on track, and by doing it consistently over the years. I originally met Cheryl is 1985. It is now 2000. I recently contacted Cheryl and asked if she would meet with me to discuss what being a wife has been like over the past 15 years. When Cheryl came in she shared with me a startling story of an event in her marriage that highlighted how far she had come in her personal development as a married woman. I was not expecting what she told me.

Cheryl told me of a terrible auto accident she was in two years ago. She was alone in her car driving through an intersection. The light was green. From out of nowhere, a car slammed into her, striking her car at the driver's door. Although Cheryl was wearing a seat belt, she was seriously injured. She suffered a broken left forearm and collarbone, but the serious injury was to her head. Apparently, her head was thrown sideways impacting the driver's side window that was simultaneously smashed against the side of her face by the force of the other car's impact. She was transported to a local hospital and put into intensive care while the staff patched her broken bones and drained fluids from her swollen and cracked skull. She was comatose for two days in a life and death struggle. It was during the comatose state that Cheryl related an interesting and, in some ways, strange story.

Apparently, within hours after her admittance to intensive care, Ed, her husband, came to her bedside. Cheryl was comatose and the doctors told him she might not recover from her injuries and could die. Ed went up to her and whispered in Cheryl's ear, "I'm here for you." He took her free hand and squeezed it. Unexpectedly, when he squeezed her hand, she squeezed his hand back! All the monitors hooked to Cheryl, at that moment, recorded increased activity. The doctors were bewildered by this: How could she have acknowledged a hand squeeze in such a near death stage and with her brain so badly traumatized? They had no answer. However, Cheryl did and she shared it with me.

"It was like deep within the recesses of my being I knew Ed was there. I felt a great surge of love for him. I wanted him to know that. So, I squeezed his hand," Cheryl said.

"But, how could you have even known he was there? How could you process his presence and your love and your desire to express it to him, and then find a neural pathway from your brain to your hand, in your comatose state?" I asked.

"Oh, I don't think it came from so much a physical place. I think squeezing his hand came from a spiritual/physical place. It came from where my love for him lies. That's the force I felt. I'm his wife, I love him; I've loved him for nearly twenty-five years. It's like my love found a spiritual place to reside in my body. It was present, and comatose or not comatose, it was from there that I was able to squeeze his hand" Cheryl explained.

"Okay, let me see if I can understand this. You're saying that you have loved Ed so deeply and so long, that your love found a physical resting place in your body. That your love has its own pathway within the body and it can express itself even through the fog of a coma. That you didn't will your hand to squeeze his along so much a physical route but mostly from a spiritual one. Right?"

"That's what I think, yes. I know it sounds sort of woo-woo, but that's what happened."

"Let me ask you a question about this. How did you develop the sort of love you are describing? It's a pretty amazing idea. I like it. I think a lot of people would like to love that way. Although, I don't recommend they discover it in intensive care! Any idea how you developed the kind of physical/spiritual loving you're describing?"

"You know, when you called and asked me to come in to talk to you about my marriage, knowing I would tell you about my accident and squeezing Ed's hand, I knew you would end up asking me something like that. I remember us talking years ago about, it's my choice to be a married, and that I must follow my values in order to be true to myself in order to find fulfillment. I've been doing that since the day you and I worked out my list. Some days I was conscious of working on it, other days I wasn't. I think being on track, as you called it, seeped into me. It became me. Overtime, I became less and less connected to Ed in reactionary ways, but more and more in the positive ways of my values. This gave me the space to love him for who he is, to accept him as a real person. Loving him in an accepting way also seemed to let me love myself in an accepting way, too. It's like they go hand in hand. Oh, we would argue at times—I don't know if you remember but Ed and I hardly ever argued, we were mostly the silent smoldering types—but the arguments were different. It was like I would sincerely say what I thought and he would too, and I had no trouble hearing him but also disagreeing with him. It didn't get out of hand. I could still love him and disagree with him. I think I learned to love him through my values and not in reaction to what he was like or not like. As time went by, I feel I became real as a wife, you know, not fake, not phony, not pretending, but really real. When I became real, I could really love! When I first came to see you, I didn't know this was possible, but I do now. I know how to love, be loved, and to love myself. When I was laying there in a coma with all those tubes hooked up to me and monitors beeping, I was physically beat up but my love wasn't. I think if I had died, I still would have found a way of letting Ed know I loved him. I know that sounds strange, but during my rehabilitation, I had a lot of time to think about this and understand it," Cheryl said.

"Wow, Cheryl, I had forgotten how thoroughly you think about things and sort them out. Are you sure you don't want to exchange chairs with me. Maybe you should be sitting here!"

"No, no, you stay just where you are. I like the seat I'm in," Cheryl said with a laugh.

"Cheryl, would it be too inane, after the deeply moving experience you've shared with me, to go over your action values and rate them? I'm curious how you see them after 15 years, and how you would rate yourself now."

"It's been a long time since I've done a rating. I've looked at the list occasionally, and I think about it a lot. Rating myself might be interesting. Sure, why not?"

"I have a copy from your file. Remember the rating scale, -3 -2 -1 0 +1 +2 +3 and the question, 'How well have you been doing being the married woman you want to be, no matter to whom you would be married?' The question helps you focus on yourself and your philosophy separate from the particular person to whom you are married," I stated.

"It's all coming back to me. Now that we are talking, it doesn't really seem that long ago that we did this," Cheryl said.

"Let's start with 'loving.' How well have you been 'loving' the way you want to be loving, being the married woman you want to be?" I asked.

"I'll rate that a +2," Cheryl stated.

"How about 'faithful'," I asked.

Cheryl said, "I'll give that a +3. Being faithful is either a +3 or -3, it seems to me. I've never even thought about not being faithful in my marriage to Ed. That's a value that has always been rock solid."

"Next, is 'positive.' How have you done with being positive." I asked.

"Let's give that a +2," Cheryl said.

Oddly enough, as we went through Cheryl's list of action values, she gave all of them, with the exception of faithful, a plus +2. All her ratings looked like this.

CHERYL RATES HER ACTION VALUES

Loving	+2	Faithful	+3
Positive	+2	Trusting	+2
Accepting	+2	Express Feelings and thoughts	+2
Respectful	+2	Good Listener	+2
Affectionate	+2	Sexual	+2
Romantic	+2	A friend	+2
Nice	+2		

From what she had told me about the emotional impact the accident had on her as a married woman, and her feelings overall about her marriage with Ed, I thought she would give herself a lot +3's. I asked her about this.

"I think I'm doing great as a wife. As we go over the list and I reflect on myself in the marriage, I am proud of what I have accomplished. I remember how I felt when I first came to see you years ago. There is no comparison with how bad I felt then and how good I feel now. But, I think I understand better now, what a +3 rating means. I know I will continue to grow and get better and better at being on track. I think a +2 is terrific. It means I'm doing a darn good job of being on track. But, I like the idea of leaving room to improve. I know that if I rate myself a +2 on being loving, that I have room to become more loving as a wife as I grow more and more as a person. I'll be working on getting to +3's all my marital life. Maybe when I become a wise, old woman, I'll feel OK about giving myself +3's. Right now, +2's say it for me. I feel great about myself now, but I know from experience, that I can always improve, that I can always add to my feelings of fulfillment in my marriage, and I can always feel more connected to Ed. In 15 years, I've changed so much that I know I will change even more. Giving myself +3's would sort of say, it's all over, I'm as good as I can get, and I don't think that's the case."

"So, we'll meet again in 15 years, Cheryl, to see what a +2 and a +3 means. I'm willing," I said. Cheryl just laughed.

"Cheryl, have there been times when you are off track?" I asked. "Times when, if you rated yourself, you would give yourself minus scores."

"No, I don't think so. There are times when I'm not on track as well as I would like, but I don't think I actually get off track anymore, you know, go into the minus range. I'm just not reactionary like I was early in the marriage. I used to think it was a federal case if I wasn't getting my way, or if Ed got moody about his business. Now, I appreciate our differences and don't feel threatened by them. When Ed and I talk about this, we like to say, 'he likes a beer and I like a glass of wine, no big deal.' I still remember what you used to say about being on track." I interrupted and we both ended up saying in unison, "A husband can make it hard or easy for you to be on track but he'll never be in charge of whether you are or not." We both got a big laugh out of expressing this mantra simultaneously.

"I'm not surprised you remember that idea, Cheryl." I said.

"It made sense at the time and it has stayed with me. There have been many occasions where reminding myself helped me through a tight spot," Cheryl replied.

"Cheryl, let me ask you about one of your action values in particular. You rated yourself a +2 on 'expressing feelings and thoughts.' In telling me about your marriage with Ed, you shared that you argue with him now, and I remember when I first met you, that you rarely openly disagreed. Back then, you said you yelled at him a few times out of frustration, but mostly you withheld your opinion. What's changed that you argue more with Ed and how is arguing Okay?" I asked.

"That's a good one," Cheryl said. "You're right, I used to be afraid to bring something up with Ed if I thought it would upset him. I would just keep quiet and stuff it and hope the issue would go away. When I got really frustrated, I yelled. Not anymore. That didn't work. Back then, I had no confidence that I could stay on track. Now, I know that no matter what, I can stay on track so I am no longer afraid of issues that we disagree about. If we disagree, I stay on track. That makes disagreeing a whole different experience. I'm strong-minded, but not stubborn. I say what I think. I listen. I remain respectful of Ed as a person who has a right to his opinion. I know how to take time-out if I have to, although rarely have I needed to. I don't think arguing is bad anymore. It's just two people expressing a difference of opinion. It's necessary. I can't imagine being married without expressing what I think. I just don't live in fear anymore of Ed's reaction, nor of mine. I know if I can remain true to my values, I can bring up anything I want with Ed. Being on track is really what makes this work. If you get off track, forget it, whatever you disagree about won't work. You'll just get stuck and frustrated. I'm glad you brought this up. I think it is one of the biggest changes I've made, and I'm so glad I made it."

"I'm glad you made the change, too. People who hide from disagreement don't seem to me to grow much as individuals. Can you imagine how boring it would be if we were all alike?" I stated.

"Cheryl, there is another area of marriage you have mentioned that I'm wondering about. You are describing a very close and sometimes intense connection with Ed. Can you talk about this closeness and how it has come about?" I asked.

Cheryl paused for a moment and said, "When I squeezed Ed's hand, I never felt so connected to another human being in my life as I did at that moment. I know that sounds strange since I was in a coma. It's like a special moment in time occurred and I was touching him and he was touching me and that's all there was to existence at the moment. I've felt the same connection with Ed since. I think since we had such a connection occur, we know it's possible, so now it can happen. It's like the discovery of it, and knowing it can happen, makes it possible. Not always. Just sometimes a special moment will occur and I feel like I am a totally alive person in the presence of another totally alive person. It's hard to explain. I read somewhere about 'peak experiences.' I think that's what it is—it's as close as I can feel to another person. Does that sound too corny?" Cheryl said.

"No, not at all." I said. "I am especially intrigued by the notion that, now that you know the peak experience of what I call the 'inter-human' can occur, that it can occur. That's true of so many things, isn't it?

"That's a term I don't remember you telling me about. What is it again?" Cheryl asked.

"It's called the inter-human, when one person connects with another with open and unconditional regard for the other as a person. Supposedly, when this happens an I-thou relationship can occur. For instance in a marriage, if an I-thou relationship unfolds between a wife and husband, they evolve a marital "inbetween" in which each fully blossoms at that moment as a human being. It's a philosophy about how we find out who we truly are as human beings in moments of mutual presence with another. The ultimate knowing of our humanness comes about in an I-thou relationship."

"Well, that's pretty heavy for me. I think I'll stick with just being a wife and stay on track as best I can," Cheryl said, smiling.

"And, well you should, Cheryl. When you came in years ago, you were feeling pretty miserable and hopeless about your marriage. Now, you know how to be on track with yourself, you're doing it, and it's brought you a lot of pride and fulfillment. I can't think of anything better than you just continuing to be who you are and do what you're doing. I truly wish you the very best," I said.

"I've got a surprise for you," Cheryl said. At that, she asked me to come out to her car. "Ed dropped me off here. He's picking me up. I'd like you to meet him."

Ed saw me coming out of the office with Cheryl. He got out of the car with a smile on his face. Not a big man, around six feet, but solid. Dressed casually, he shook my hand firmly. Against my "indoor hand," his felt strong and callused. I liked him immediately. Cheryl introduced us.

"It's nice meeting you, Ed," I said. "You're a lucky man. I admire Cheryl a lot."

"Not as much as I do," he said. We all three laughed. "Thanks for what you've done for our marriage."

"You're welcome," I said, "but thanks must go to Cheryl. She did all the hard work. I just talked a lot and listened. I'm very glad your marriage is going so well. I wish you much continued happiness."

We chatted for a few minutes, and then they drove off. It was a good feeling meeting Ed, and seeing Cheryl with her husband. It made her marriage more real to me.

I am very impressed with what Cheryl accomplished as a married woman. My wish for her is the same that I have for all women who choose to be married and read this book—that you not only figure out how to be married successfully, but also that you reach your potential as a married woman. That you become your higher self, experience fulfillment, and attain a full sense of your own humanness in your marital relationship with your husband, as Cheryl did.

PART EIGHT: A CONCLUDING PRIMER

A number of married women have read and reviewed preliminary copies of this book. They told me that each time they read sections of the book, they found more and more ideas useful to them as disparate issues came up in their marital experience to which principles in the book apply. They said that the book is more complex than it seems. In order to help with this complexity, they suggested that I conclude the book with a concise overview in the form of a primer that they could review and copy and keep handy as a reminder of how to effectively guide themselves in marriage. So, what follows is a primer on what a you need to know to accomplish a marriage makeover and become a new and better marital you.

THE MARRIED WOMAN

**MARRIAGE MAKEOVER
STEP TWENTY-TWO**

An Overview

*A primer on how a
married woman can have a new
and better start in being married.*

<u>Be an adult woman who is choosing to be married.</u> Take responsibility for your choice to be married. No one can make you be married but you. Once you have acknowledged your choice, commit yourself to making it work for you. It will never make sense to choose to be married and then go about it in a way that obviously will never work. Find out how to be married successfully and do it.

<u>Be your color.</u> A marriage is composed of you, the wife, your spouse, the husband, and your mutually created marital inbetween. You are in charge of your choice to be a married woman and your participation (color) in the marital inbetween, that's it. Your husband can make it hard or easy for you to be your color, but he will never be in charge of what color you choose to be. You are not in charge of your husband's choice to be a married man or his participation (color) either, only he is. Putting the best of your action values—your color—into the marital inbetween is the most you can do to increase the quality of your mar-

riage. All your power to feel pride and fulfillment as a married woman comes from your color.

Acknowledge that your choice to be married is conditional. You don't stop being a rational and reasonable adult woman when you get married. There always could be activities or events in your marriage that might occur, and if so, it would be reasonable for you to get a divorce and unreasonable to stay married. Your choice to be a wife is conditional, as it should be. That's normal and wise. Mature adults do not enter into unconditional relationships. Remember though, conditions apply to your choice to be married, not to your husband's behavior. He is an adult and can do whatever in life he chooses. It may be that no woman of personal value will be married to him, but that does not negate his right to be who he is. Don't give ultimatums. Instead, express conditions that apply to your choice to be married or not. If conditions do not exist, then whatever is bugging you is a problem to work on and not a condition over which to divorce..

Promise to try to solve problems in your marriage. Problems go with your marital territory. Commit yourself to problem solving. Promise yourself that you will always do everything in your power to try to solve whatever problems emerge in your marriage before letting yourself think of divorce. Never think of divorce unless you are convinced you are dealing with a condition. Problems can be solved or lived with. Don't run from problems. Don't ignore problems. Do something about them. Marriages in which one spouse gets frustrated and says, "I want out of here," (referring to the marriage) don't work. Marriages in which a spouse gets frustrated and asks, "Have I done everything possible to solve or find a way to live with this problem?" are creative and promise-solution marriages that do work. Remember, if it is not a condition, it is a problem to try to solve.

Be faithful. Don't have affairs. Affairs require lying and deceit. You can't bring dishonesty and deceit into your marriage and expect to have a good one. No one makes you be married, but you. Wherever you go take your "wife sphere" with you. You are a married woman wherever you go: at work, on a trip, in a bar or restaurant, when out with the "girls." Draw your wife sphere boundaries between yourself and others so that your values and wisdom are present. Don't draw the line where someone else may want you to draw it, i.e., flirting, talking intimately, exploring sexual availability, rubbing bodies, or in bed. You can be friends with the opposite sex, but don't let yourself try to get him to meet your intimacy needs nor to meet his needs for inappropriate closeness. Be true to your choice to be married. Be faithful.

Love without ifs. Make your love for your spouse non-iffy. He doesn't have to do anything to earn it. Your love is non-contingent. It has nothing to do with whether he is upbeat or on a downer, fat or skinny, handsome or ugly, successful or unsuccessful, a good guy or a bad guy at the moment. Connect your loving feelings to the choice you've made to be married. As long as you choose to be married, love him without ifs. Take charge of nurturing and maintaining your love—own your love! Hold it in your heart and give it to him without reservation. This kind of loving requires that you be fully human and in your humanness and the loving that comes from it, you can experience the best of who you are. It may take time and effort to get to this kind of loving, but it's worth it, for you and for your spouse. Make it your goal to be a married woman who loves freely. Bring non-iffy loving through you to your marriage.

Get on track being the wife you want to be. Be in charge of what you are like as a married woman. Don't put your reactions to your husband in charge of what you are like as a spouse. Create a place of wisdom in your mind—a compartment called mindfulness—from which you can guide yourself. Enclose in this space of wisdom your action values for what you want to be like as a married woman. Guide yourself by these action values. This is called being "on track." Your husband can make it hard or easy for you to be on track, but he will never be in charge of whether or not you are on track. You are! Know your action values. Be your action values. Great fulfillment as a married woman awaits you as you get better at being on track.

Get back on track if you get off. Everybody gets off track. Don't waste energy criticizing yourself for getting off track, instead focus your efforts on getting back on track. Get good at this.

Think positive thoughts about your husband. Make every assumption in your mind about your husband into a positive statement. He isn't late; he got home as soon as he could. He isn't ignoring you; he is doing his best to manage his worries and energy for attention. Don't let yourself indulge in angry, frustrating, irritating negative thinking and blaming scenarios about him in your mind. No matter how much negative thinking you allow yourself to indulge, chances are you will still lie next to him in bed at night, get up with him in the morning and continue on with demands of the next day. Negative thinking only makes it harder for you to be married to him and to stay on track. You are married to an adult man doing his best in a complex and demanding world. He's not going to be perfect and neither are you. Doing well is not easy for him. Doing well is not easy for you. Be generous and forgiving. Live with grace. Assume he is doing his best. While we are on the subject of thinking positive thoughts about your spouse, let me say that you will benefit from taking this generous and forgiving attitude toward yourself, as well. It shows that, as a rational, intelligent woman, you have recognized that perfection is not all it is cracked up to be for you or for him.

Guide yourself by feeling, thinking and acting. Know the difference between feelings and actions. We all feel and we all act. Many of us believe that if we have a feeling and act directly on it we are being authentic. My husband ignores me, I feel hurt, so I must withdraw because pulling away from him emotionally is consistent with the way I feel. Many situations in life work better for us—produce pride and confidence—when we act in ways we believe to be right despite feelings to the contrary. Instead of withdrawing, you remain on track—you don't put the feelings inspired by your husband ignoring you in charge of what you are like as a married woman. This helps you be successful as a wife. It helps you be married successfully. This is what is called, feel-THINK-act, as opposed to, feel-ACT-think. One works, the other doesn't. It works to be aware of your values for yourself and not to just act purely out of emotion.

Guide yourself from your action values. If you don't guide your actions exclusively from your feelings, where do you focus for guidance? The answer is: Your action values. You know what you want to be like as a spouse. You've thought about it; you've got your list. You know if you want to be a good listener, expressive, understanding, accepting, and affectionate. You know what being a good listener means to you—if has a very personal meaning. You know, too, what it looks like when you are being expressive, understanding, accepting, and affectionate. You have thought about your action values and the behaviors embodied in them. You know you are in charge of them. You know that your husband can make it hard or easy for you to be on track with your action values. And, you know that in order to feel proud and fulfilled as a wife, you must guide yourself from your action values and not from negative emotional reactions to your husband. Knowing how to separate what you feel like doing from what you are going to do—separate feelings from actions and then guiding yourself from your action values—puts you in charge of your self-regard as a married woman.

Make the main job in your marriage being on track as the married woman you want to be. This may sound a bit one-dimensional but if you recall the structure of marriage it makes a lot of sense. What you are in charge of is the choice to be married and how you participate in your marriage—whether you are on track as the spouse you want to be. The most you can do about any qualitative aspect of your marriage is to manage what you put into the mutually constituted marital sphere by consistently putting into the marital inbetween your best color. It is not your job to make your husband happy, to feel good about himself, nor to feel fulfilled in life. These are all jobs that exist in his domain, just as they do in yours. Can you contribute to his happiness, self-esteem and fulfillment (and he to yours)? You bet! How so? By being on track. By putting the best of your color into the marital inbetween. When you are on track with your action values, you are putting the best of yourself into the marriage sphere. He experiences YOU and the marriage in this sphere. The experience he can have of you being the best you can be, is the most he can get from you, that can be helpful to him in his desire to feel good about himself and fulfilled as a husband and a person.

So make being the married woman you want to be—being on track with your action values—your main job in the marriage. Trust that you are exercising all the real power you have over all aspects of the marital inbetween (and whatever either of you will get from it that is helpful to you in life) by being on track. It's a win-win approach to being married—you both get the most that is possible out of the mix of the marital inbetween by what you put into it through YOUR efforts to be on track.

<u>*Reach for your higher self*</u>. Knowing how to be on track creates great potential for you as a married woman. As you stay on track as the married woman you want to be, you can get better and better at being your higher self as a wife—a woman who is her very best color as a spouse. Overtime, you will be able to experience more and more satisfaction and pride in yourself as a married woman. Being your very best color can bring you feelings of self-actualization—the awareness that you are

doing a very good job as the wife you want to be. As this happens, you are able to feel more and more fulfillment as a married woman. You will be able to realize that you have made a choice to be a married woman and the choice is filled up with inner joy at how well you have done it. My wish for you is that you extend yourself as far as you can, and reach as much of your potential that possibly can be attained as a married woman, and that your marriage makeover helps you get there.

The Married Man

The next book in Dr. Bradley's series on marriage, *Marriage Overhaul: A Man's Guide to a Better Marriage,* will be published in 2002.

The Married Man is for the husband in a troubled marriage, who doesn't want a divorce, but wants to feel successful and fulfilled as a married man. He feels stuck and he doesn't know what to do. He may be hurt, angry, disheartened or bewildered. He wants to be married and feel better. *The Married Man* explains what a husband can do through his own efforts to so change the way he is going about being married, that he regains feelings of hope for himself and his marriage. Through straightforward explanations, examples of other men's struggles and successes, and practical skills, he learns to take responsibility for his choice to be married, and how to become an action valued married man in charge of his self-regard as a husband. He also acquires tips for how to de-escalate arguments, resolve resentments, divide up household tasks, support individual interests, differentiate being a father and husband, and maintain romance. Ultimately, the book helps the married man realize his best self in marriage. *The Married Man* is the companion book to *Marriage Makeover.* While the advice in each book addresses spouses individually, taken together the books represent a common format for a husband and wife to work on a satisfying marriage together. With the knowledge from both books, each spouse can take responsibility for how he or she participates in the marriage, and together they can create a rich and rewarding marital experience.

Printed in the United States
5768